# The Log

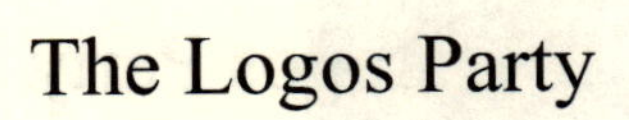

# The Logos Party

# The Logos Party

## Doctor Democracy's Remedy for Improving Political Dialogue

Dustin Lawson

The Logos Party

**ISBN:** 978-1-70707-406-8



www.logosparty.com



Printed in the United States of America

# The Logos Party

"I see the time approaching when freedom, public peace, and social order itself will not be able to do without enlightenment."

-Alexis de Tocqueville
(*Democracy in America)*

# Table of Contents

# Introduction

## McCain-Lieberman 2008: The Bipartisan Revolution America Almost Had

In 2008 the United States elected its first African American president, Barack Hussein Obama. It was a political revolution in racial diversity that was long overdue. But I think the 2008 presidential campaign almost gave America an even greater political revolution in a different and more important type of diversity: intellectual diversity.[1]

As the Republican nominee for President of the United States, Senator John McCain probably believed that if he was going to beat Senator Obama, he had to do something unprecedented when choosing a running mate. For McCain, bold choices were nothing new. That is why he was nicknamed "Maverick." But McCain's first choice for his running mate was maybe the boldest decision of his political career. His first choice was his good friend, Senator Joe Lieberman, a Democrat.[2]

At the founding of the United States, the person who received the second most electoral votes

---

[1] Being able to embrace racial diversity, or any other type of diversity, is dependent on intellectual diversity being embraced.

[2] Lieberman was officially registered as an "independent Democrat."

became the vice president. This worked fine for George Washington's two terms (1789-1797) because he ran unopposed in both elections. That meant his vice president, John Adams, wasn't someone who had been his opponent, which could have made the relationship more contentious. It was also before the existence of established political parties. A United States without parties did not last long.

By the third presidential election in 1796, two opposing major political parties had been formed: The Federalists and the Democratic-Republicans. The winner was John Adams, the Federalists candidate. The person with the second most electoral votes was Thomas Jefferson, the Democratic-Republican's candidate and Adam's bitter partisan rival. Jefferson served as Adams's vice president. But, after only one term, Jefferson ran against Adams and beat him.

As a result, the country began to think that maybe it wasn't realistic for the president and vice president to be from opposing parties. In 1804 the 12th Amendment to the Constitution was ratified, paving the way for presidents being able to choose their own vice presidents. Since then, besides Republican Lincoln choosing Democrat Johnson as his vice president in 1864, every president has chosen a running mate from his own party.

By having a Republican-Democrat ticket, Senator McCain could have helped break through partisan barriers and shown the country that Republicans and Democrats should not see each other as enemies. Instead, because different opinions working together in a culture of intellectual diversity was good for the country, they should be allies. As

Thomas Jefferson wrote, "Difference of opinion leads to enquiry, and enquiry to truth."[3]

By choosing Lieberman, McCain could have helped foster a reason-based political culture of intellectual diversity within the two-party system. Within this culture, Republicans and Democrats could agree that neither party is always right or always wrong, sometimes a Republican has a better idea than a Democrat, sometimes a Democrat has a better idea than a Republican, sometimes neither side has a good idea, and they might need to look outside of the two-party system for answers. As John F. Kennedy wrote, "Let us not seek the Republican answer or the Democratic answer, but the right answer."[4]

Throughout his career, McCain made a habit of reaching across the aisle and working with Democrats. In his last book, *The Restless Wave*, McCain wrote, "Principled compromises...can be found when we put political advantage slightly second to the problem we're trying to solve. Muddling through, hashing out policy agreements that thrill no one but are acceptable to most, is a useful achievement in a republic." Because of his willingness to work with people with whom he disagreed, McCain called himself a "champion of compromise."

But compromise had to be mutual. By wanting Lieberman as a running mate, McCain was willing to give Democrats the keys to the White House if he died or became incapacitated while serving as president. But McCain wasn't willing to give that opportunity to just any Democrat. There was something that McCain and Lieberman shared that was more important than

---

[3] Jefferson wrote this line in a letter to Peter H. Wendover on 13 March 1815.

[4] JFK said this line in a speech at Loyola College Alumni Banquet in Baltimore, Maryland on February 18, 1958.

the differences in their political platforms. I believe what McCain viewed as more important was the shared foundation of values on which they built their platforms.[5] Even though they disagreed on a lot, because of their shared values, McCain trusted Lieberman to have the country's best interest in mind and, if something happened to him, McCain trusted that Lieberman would also reach across the aisle and work with Republicans, instead of working from a foundation of partisan dogma that prohibited him from making principled compromises with the other side.

If McCain had chosen Lieberman as his running mate and won, the United States would have had an example of a bipartisan White House for at least four years and probably eight years, which might have revolutionized the two-party system for a generation, if not longer. This revolution could have broken through partisan dogma and caused the two major parties to truly see each other as allies on the journey towards greater enlightenment.

***

Unfortunately, the United States never benefited from this example of bipartisanship. Once word got out that McCain wanted Lieberman, Republican leaders threatened to revolt.[6] Frustrated with his party, McCain eventually gave in to the

---

[5] John McCain is no longer alive to verify or challenge what I write about him. So, out of respect for the dead, I admit I could be partly or completely wrong about his reasons for wanting Lieberman as his running mate.

[6] Many Democrats would have rejoiced in the idea of a McCain-Lieberman ticket. But if the roles had been reversed and Lieberman was their nominee for president and wanted to choose McCain as his running mate, most Democrats probably would have threatened the same revolt the Republicans did.

pressure and settled on the Republican governor of Alaska, Sarah Palin.

Palin helped advance a culture of passionate anti-intellectualism that furthered the political culture of extreme partisanship. As a result, instead of the Republican Party continuing to be (at least partly) symbolized by intellectual giants like Abraham Lincoln and Teddy Roosevelt whom McCain tried to emulate, it was branded by dogmatic partisanship, divisiveness, censorship, resentment towards criticism, and a belief that anyone with a different opinion is always wrong and evil.[7]

During the 2008 presidential campaign, I was an Independent because I could not bring myself to join a party that expected me to fall in line with them ideologically on every issue, and might have asked me to leave the party if I changed my mind. But if McCain had chosen Lieberman as his running mate and won, I would have been ready to join the Republican Party. Since that didn't happen, I remained an Independent and have been one ever since.

***

I had the privilege of meeting Senator McCain in 2017. I was deployed as a public affairs officer with the Army National Guard in the country of Kosovo. McCain was visiting many countries in the Balkans to help strengthen NATO alliances. Kosovo was one of his stops.

Alongside my Commander and Sergeant Major, I flew in a Blackhawk helicopter from Camp Bondsteel to Pristina International Airport to greet Senator

---

[7] Before he died, in an HBO documentary called "For Whom the Bell Tolls", McCain said he regretted not choosing Lieberman.

McCain. When the Senator deplaned, before greeting my Commander, he walked to the wing and tapped a dent. Smiling, he looked back and said, "We hit a bird. Shook the plane. But I've been in planes that have been hit by worse."

On the cramped Blackhawk ride from the airport back to Camp Bondsteel, I couldn't help but sneak a look at McCain's crooked fingers, which had been broken while he was a prisoner of war. At Camp Bondsteel, McCain spoke in Audie Murphy Medal of Honor Hall to an auditorium full of soldiers, then had a luncheon in the VIP cafeteria room with a select group of soldiers and civilians. Afterwards, the Senator posed for pictures. I was the photographer. One person, when they stepped up to get their picture with the Senator, said, "I voted for you."

"So many people tell me that it makes me wonder how I lost," McCain joked.

I almost said, "If you had picked Lieberman as your running mate you probably would have won," but I held my tongue.

It was a couple months later when McCain had the surgery to remove a blood clot above his eye. The world would soon find out it was caused by stage four brain cancer.

***

When Senator McCain died, my roommate from the Kosovo deployment—who spent more time with McCain than I had because he was the deployment's VIP escort—flew from Michigan to Washington to go to the Capitol Building with me to see McCain lay in state.[8]

---

[8] At this point in my career, I had accepted a White House-appointed position in Washington D.C. as a speechwriter for the

I took this opportunity to show my friend around the city before going to the Capitol Building. We went to the National Archives. I had not been to the Archives in nine years. When we stepped into the Rotunda, I noticed that the room was much dimmer than I remembered. When I saw the Declaration of Independence and the Constitution, I gasped as I realized why: the founding documents had faded substantially. The Archives were trying to prevent fading by reducing the amount of light that fell on the documents.

Looking at the mostly illegible Declaration of Independence and barely legible Constitution, I was reminded of the spell in *Beauty and the Beast:* If the prince could not fall in love before the last enchanted rose petal fell, the curse would never lift. Similarly, I imagined America's democracy under a spell that caused it to gradually die as the founding documents gradually faded, and, if the founding documents ever completely faded, the United States' democracy would cease to exist altogether.

After the Archives visit, my friend and I stood in line for three hours in the summer heat on 1st Street, which separates the Supreme Court and the Library of Congress from the Capitol Building. It was so hot, some people passed out and had to be carried out of line into the shade.

Eventually, we made it into the air-conditioned Capitol Building and Rotunda. Like everyone else, I solemnly stared at Senator McCain's flag-draped casket, which was guarded by stoic soldiers on each end. The longer I stared at the casket, the more it felt like something bigger had died. An idea had perished,

---

Millennium Challenge Corporation, a government agency focused on foreign development for the world's best-governed poor countries.

gradually fading like the founding documents: the idea of an intellectually diverse reason-based bipartisan political culture that viewed the preservation of a healthy democracy as more important than party loyalty.

I looked up from McCain's casket to the paintings on the Rotunda walls. I then looked up 180 feet to the top of the dome. *The Apotheosis of Washington* depicted George Washington, draped in purple, sitting in the heavens, exalted. I was reminded of President Washington's farewell address where he spoke against political parties:

> "The common and continual mischiefs of the spirit of party are sufficient to make it the interest and the duty of a wise people to discourage and restrain it. It serves always to distract the public councils and enfeeble the public administration. It agitates the community with ill-founded jealousies and false alarms, kindles the animosity of one party against another, and foments occasionally riot and insurrection. It opens the door to foreign influence and corruption, which find a facilitated access to the government itself through the channels of party passion."

There may be no truer words ever written or spoken by a president.

From his lofty perch in the dome above, it felt like President Washington was looking down at McCain's casket and saying, "He tried to restrain 'the spirit of party' I warned against. Now who is left to fight against the partisan dogma that continues to destroy the democracy I helped build?"

As more people came into the Rotunda, a security guard motioned for me to leave. I was reluctant because it felt as if as soon as I stepped out of the Rotunda, the hope of non-partisan, reason-based politics would be lost. There would be nothing that could reverse the slow death of American democracy. All we could do was watch it happen.

After leaving the Capitol, my friend and I walked around downtown. When we walked by the Archives, I was afraid if I went back in the Declaration of Independence and Constitution would be even more faded than they were earlier in the day, as if another rose petal had fallen off and American democracy was one step closer to dying.

A couple of blocks from the White House near Franklin Square, my friend and I stopped in a pizza shop. I looked at the menu for a minute, unsure of what to order. Then, the decision became easy when I saw the name of one of the pizzas. It was called "Maverick."

## Chapter One

## Doctor Democracy's Diagnosis

On December 22, almost four months after McCain's funeral, the government shut down. It remained shut down until January 25, 2019—the longest government shutdown in United States history.

While furloughed, I didn't leave Washington D.C. because I didn't know when I would receive a message telling me to come back to work the next day. So I spent most of the shutdown at my house, reading and writing.

One of the many things I read was the Democracy Index, a yearly ranking of the world's democracies based on 60 indicators in five categories.[9] The first year of the Index was 2006.[10] That year, the United States' democracy was ranked 17th and labeled a "full democracy." In 2014, our democracy was ranked 19th. In 2016, it was ranked 21st and labeled a "flawed democracy". In 2018, the United States' democracy was ranked 25th and again labeled a "flawed democracy." Our democracy is declining and has been for years.

---

[9] These categories are electoral process and pluralism, functioning of government, political participation, democratic political culture and civil liberties.

[10] I thought the Democracy Index was like an annual fitness contest where all the world's democracies compete for the title of 'world's fittest democracy.'

As a soldier, I wore armor to protect me from outside threats that could kill me quickly. American democracy also wore armor, protecting itself from outside threats through national security and diplomacy. But as a cancer survivor, [11] I understood that there were also subtle threats to my body that could slay me slowly from within. After reading the Democracy Index, I saw subtle (and obvious) threats that were slowly killing American democracy from within. When I became a soldier, I swore to protect the country from all threats, both foreign and *domestic*. During the shutdown, I began to feel that I should try to do something to help protect American democracy from the domestic threats that were hurting the health of the Republic from within.

But self-doubt creeped in. *What can I do? I have no position of power. I am just a common citizen who grew up in rural Ohio. I have some military experience, a little bit of government experience, and my experience as a writer, but I don't specialize in the health of democracies.* I then had an idea: I didn't specialize in the health of democracy, but I could create someone who did.[12]

There was a knock at my door.

I looked out the window. Standing on my front porch was a middle-aged man dressed in scrubs and a long white lab coat. I opened the door a couple inches and asked, "Can I help you with something?"

The man said, "Actually, I think I can help you. I hear you are looking for help improving the health of American democracy. I had some time between

---

[11] My cancer was found at stage one and surgery was all that was needed to get rid of it.

[12] When writing novels I sometimes like to imagine the characters sitting with me as I write.

checkups in Europe and Asia, and the United States is long overdue, so I thought I would stop by."

I asked, "Who are you?"

"Oh, sorry," the man said as he held out his hand. "I'm Doctor Democracy. I was first hired by the Founding Fathers during the Constitutional Convention in 1787 to give regular checkups to America's young Republic. But, as the United States grew in size and strength throughout the 19th and 20th centuries, especially after the fall of the Soviet Union, you began to feel invincible and decided you no longer needed regular checkups. You began to avoid me and eventually stopped seeing me altogether. After the end of the Cold War, as I was no longer employed by the United States, I was hired by other countries, mostly democracies who now outrank the United States."

Unwilling to shake the man's hand, I asked, "The Founding Fathers hired you? So, you are hundreds of years old?"

Doctor Democracy lowered his hand. "I understand this is difficult to believe. When the Founding Fathers hired me, I was the embodiment of all the great political and philosophical thinkers of history—from ancient Greece to the Enlightenment—that they relied on to help them write the Declaration of Independence, the Constitution and the Bill of Rights. Once the Founding Fathers died, many of them became part of me that future leaders of the United States and other democracies relied on. Then, when people like Lincoln, Teddy Roosevelt, Eisenhower and JFK died, they also became part of me. Basically, I am the collective conscious of the great minds of political and philosophical history, tasked with teaching best health practices to the world's democracies."

The doctor shivered in the cold January air.

Though still skeptical, I opened the door. "Would you like to come in?"

Doctor Democracy stepped into my home.

I sat down at my desk and pulled a chair over for the doctor. He sat down. The doctor and my roommates cat stared at each other, almost as if the pet could see him. My roommate's cat, seemingly frightened, ran away. Then, not much for small talk, the doctor began to give me his assessment of the health of American democracy. To simplify the assessment so I could better understand it, the doctor compared the different parts of American democracy to a human body. This is a summary of the doctor's evaluation.

## The Doctor's Health Assessment

As in humans, so also the body of democracy has many systems.

1. The *skeletal system* of American democracy is the Constitution, which provides the bone structure that gives democracy its form, and the ligaments and cartilage that hold it together.

   The American Constitution has provided a strong skeletal structure for over two centuries. One of the reasons it has survived and thrived is because it was created to be a flexible document that can be adapted to fit each new generation. Each generation should interpret the Constitution within the context of their ever-changing world and consider what changes should be made to the document so that it better fits the current times. Also, the amendment process gives the body of democracy the ability to stretch, keeping it flexible and the skeletal structure strong.

Unfortunately, because of the extreme partisan nature of American politics, the Constitution is hindered from being improved upon. It hasn't stretched in quite some time. This causes the body to age faster, losing its youthful vigor that allowed it to better carry the country through the unique challenges of each generation. As a result, some of the bones of the Constitution are developing arthritis and even osteoporosis. Also, because of the partisan nature of American politics, other bones that are strong and good for the body of democracy are being stressed to the point of potentially fracturing. Parties are causing constitutional crises whenever they perceive that following the Constitution would in some way hurt their party. The party has become more important than the constitution.

2. Democracy's *nervous system*, which collects and processes information from the senses and sends messages to the body, is the free press allowed through the first amendment.

   Whether we like it or not, there are standards that must be followed for a human body to be healthy: clean air must be breathed, clean water drank, clean food eaten, regular and diverse exercise performed, and a consistent rest cycle maintained. If we break any of these standards, the health of our body begins to break down. We cannot follow a standard of health different than what the human body is made for and expect our bodies to remain healthy.

   So also the body of democracy has standards that have to be followed for it to remain healthy. The main standard is a commitment to truth. President Ford expressed this idea when he said,

"Truth is the glue that holds government together."[13]

Through the five senses, it is the function of the nervous system to bring in information and send it to the brain. The brain processes that information, organizing it and trying to send accurate messages to the entire body for how best to function in its current environment. In a healthy democracy, the nervous system of the free press brings in information from many different sources. It is then the job of the nervous system to assess all of that conflicting information before sending messages of truth throughout the body for how best to live within a democratic society. For a healthy democracy to be a government of the people, by the people, for the people, the people must receive accurate information. It is here where most of the health problems of American democracy begin.

In a healthy democracy, the free press is also supposed to be the independent press. This means, though complete objectivity is probably not realistic, that the press is supposed to be unbiased and maintain a level of separation from those they cover. Unfortunately, much of the media has taken sides and helped create the current political culture of extreme partisanship. Propaganda has always been a part of American democracy, but, through traditional media and now social media, it has become epidemic.

As a result, the political left and right brain of American democracy, instead of communicating with each other and working together to send

---

[13] President Ford said this line on November 15, 1973 during his hearing before the House Committee on the Judiciary after he was nominated to replace Spiro Agnew as Vice President of the United States.

consistent messages of truth to the body to help it stay healthy, act as if they are two separate, conflicting brains within the same skull, pulling the body in different directions through "different facts" and conflicting messages of reality. In essence, the free press has helped cause America to have multiple personality disorder.

3. The *digestive system* breaks down food so nutrients can be absorbed and solid waste eliminated, while the *excretory system* filters fluids. In the body of a healthy democracy, these systems are the consciousness of the citizenry. Once the nervous system of the free press decides what is edible and drinkable, the digestive and excretory systems use reason to separate the nutrients (truth) from the waste (the false).

   Unfortunately, democracy's digestive system is struggling to determine the nutritious truth because a large portion of the citizenry do not practice critical thinking. They absorb much of what is false and excrete much truth. As a result, it is becoming more difficult for the body to distinguish the real from the false.

   If a person feeds his body bad food, his body may at first reject the food by getting sick. But, if that person continues to feed his body bad food, his body may grow used to it. So, instead of rejecting the bad food, his body begins absorbing it. As a result, the body's health slowly declines. Likewise, the body of democracy may at first reject the false nutrition that one of the two minds feeds it by growing sick. But, as time goes on, and the body is not receiving nutritious truth, it may begin adapting, absorbing the false information as reality. The body of democracy stays healthy on truth alone. So, even though it may adapt or become addicted to false information and pull whatever nutrition it can from it, the health of the democracy still gradually declines.

4. The *exocrine system* of American democracy, the glands that produce and secrete substances that lubricate the body, is a culture of compromise. Earlier, I quoted President Ford as saying, "Truth is the glue that holds government together." The second part of that quote is, "Compromise is the oil that makes governments go." Lubrication keeps the body moving efficiently. Likewise, a culture of compromise between different political groups keeps a healthy democracy's progress moving forward. This culture of compromise is also the fluid that lubricates the joints, helping the Constitution maintain a wide range of movement so it is adaptable to each generation.

    The dogmatic nature of American politics has caused a drastic decline in its culture of compromise. Instead, parties tend to view compromise as evil. As a result, the progress within a democracy grinds to a halt, and the body ages more quickly.

5. Elections represent the *respiratory system*. The Constitution gives democracy its form and holds everything together, but it is elections that breathe life into the body. As the human body must regularly breathe, so also free and fair elections should be regular.

    Elections in American democracy are regular, so the body is still consistently breathing. The more people who vote across all sectors of society, the bigger the breath democracy can take in. Political participation fluctuates depending on the election and the candidates, but there is still a far lower percentage of people participating in elections than what a healthy democracy should have. Thomas Jefferson supposedly wrote, "We in America do not have government by the majority. We have government by the majority who participate."[14]

The body of democracy regularly breaths through free and fair elections, but the air is polluted because of toxic partisanship. Both groups poison elections through things like gerrymandering and prejudicial election laws. And, because of the need to raise large amounts of money, not all citizens have an equal opportunity to run for office, further hurting the fairness of the election process.

Because of the poor quality of air, our lungs look much older than they should. American democracy has lost much of its endurance, barely able to walk upstairs without losing its breath.

6. The people who participate in democracy are the *circulatory system*. The citizens who participate in elections and civil society are the blood and heart of democracy itself.[15]

   The heart of democracy is still strong, but nowhere near as strong as it could be. Also, we've got circulation problems. The more people participate as informed citizens, the better the circulation. But because of partisan politics, large

[14] This quote is often attributed to Jefferson, but this is also disputed because it does not seem to be found in any of his writings.

[15] The digestive and excretory system are the consciousness of the entire citizenry, everyone who absorbs information from the free press. The circulatory system is only those citizens who participate in democracy by voting and being active in civil society.

portions of the people do not stay accurately and widely informed. To improve circulation and prevent blood clots, democracy requires a love of intellectual diversity and the practice of critical thinking.

7. The *muscular system* is represented by the elected officials in the executive and legislative branches, as well as the national, state and local governments, who ensure all muscle groups are strong.

When in good health, the body of a democracy looks like that of an Olympic gymnast: muscularly proportioned, agile, able to perform many different routines with strength and endurance. That is not what the body of American democracy looks like today.

The body of American democracy looks bulky with little definition because the federal government—the big muscles groups—continue to pull more and more power from the states, giving less attention to the smaller muscles, making the states more and more dependent on the federal government.

The goal of America's current political system is not muscular proportion, strength or endurance. Rather, the left and the right, when they are in power, only want to work out their side of the body, hoping the other side will atrophy. Meanwhile, both sides usually neglect the more important muscles, the core muscles of common ground and compromise that are the foundation of strength. Both sides seem blind to the reality that strong core muscles helps the whole body become stronger.

Instead of working out together to improve the health of American democracy, the left and the right often arm wrestle with each other. That is at least some physical activity. But now, the two sides have resorted to choking their own body, trying to cut off oxygen to the other side and kill it, not realizing that this will only kill the entire democracy.

8. The *immune system* is the rule of law and the judicial system. Sickness may enter the body, but a healthy immune system can fight off disease. The immune system within a healthy democracy continuously builds resistance to fight any illness by enforcing laws, creating new laws, and eliminating or amending bad laws.

   The immune system of American democracy is still strong. That said, the American judicial system has always had struggles with enforcing equal justice under the law across different classes, genders, and races.

   Thought it probably still is the most respected of the three branches, in recent decades, the immune system of the federal judicial system has grown slightly weaker. Each side has tried to make the judicial system partisan in its favor, sacrificing some of its independent nature. This runs the risk of creating a weakened immune system that allows in specific illnesses with the hope that those illnesses will only be detrimental to the health of the opposition. But this hurts the entire democracy.

9. The *endocrine system*, which provides hormonal balance, is democracy's system of checks and balances. Separate and shared powers give different branches of government the authority to check the powers of each other. This maintains balance in the body of democracy.

The endocrine system of American democracy is still functional, but it is weakening. The branches of government should hold one another accountable, regardless of which party is in power in the White House or on Capitol Hill. Unfortunately, partisan dogma often causes either party to be unwilling to hold their own members accountable, instead holding a double standard that allows them to overlook their own indiscretions while holding the other party to a far stricter standard. This is causing a hormonal imbalance within the body of American democracy.

That imbalance is also exacerbated by the disproportionate power between the legislative and executive branches, as the executive grows far more powerful than the legislative. The legislative branch can still check the powers of the executive, but its ability to do this is waning. And if the same party controls both the legislative and executive branches, then one branch will not hold the other accountable if they commit infractions. And the court system, as it becomes increasingly partisan, will show less willingness to check the powers of the legislative and executive branch if the party that appointed the judge is in power.

10. The *reproductive system* of democracy is the American dream, the idea that all citizens of the United States have the same fundamental rights. So—regardless of gender, race, or family name—through talent, hard work, and luck a person has the chance to achieve his or her dreams.[16] The

[16] There is a distinction between the "American Dream" and the "American reality." The dream is the idealistic version of America where everybody is supposed to have the same fundamental rights. The reality is an America where that is not entirely true.

attractive American dream has led many countries to try and reproduce the same dream.

The idealistic version of American democracy is still attractive to much of the world, but the modern version, though still attractive and a good example to follow, has lost some of its sex appeal. For all the reasons described above, dogmatic partisanship has caused American democracy's overall health and image to gradually decline. Because of extreme partisanship, American democracy would often rather fight itself than work together to continue reproducing democratic values around the world.

In 1789, when the Constitution was ratified and implemented, the United States was the only democracy in the world. So, in a way, American democracy is the patriarch of every democracy in the world today. Many of the world's democracies are beginning to think that grandpa has let himself go. And, with the patriarch's example faltering, some of the world's democracies are forgetting the lessons of history and seeing authoritarianism as a more attractive option.

## The Common Cause

After the doctor finished giving his health assessment, he leaned back in the chair and asked, "Do you see a common source for most of American democracy's health problems?"

I nodded. "The two-party system?"

---

As we look over the course of American history, there has been great progress made towards making that dream one day a reality, even if many times it seems like we take two steps forward and one step back.

Doctor Democracy shook his head. "Not exactly. The two-party system isn't inherently flawed. A two-party system like what a McCain-Lieberman White House could have inspired might have given America a healthy democracy. It is the current nature of the two-party system that is the problem, the dogma within the two-party system that is destroying the health of American democracy.

"For most of history, America's two-party system has lived partly in the gray phase of compromise and partly in the black and white phase of partisan dogma where compromise is not tolerated. But now the two-party system has eliminated most of the gray and exists almost completely in the black and white phase. In the gray phase, the two parties see each other as allies. They work together for the common good by pulling from the wisdom of their different opinions. In the black and white phase of extreme partisan dogma, they see each other as enemies to be destroyed.

"Without great examples of bipartisanship like what McCain wanted to provide, two-party systems often gravitate towards black and white extremes, where the other party is always wrong and must be defeated at any cost, even if that cost is electoral integrity, democracy, and truth. And they will justify whatever means are necessary if it will assure their candidates win and their policy platform becomes legislation. They will rarely, if ever, care about the credibility of the decision-making process they use to pick their candidates or form their policy views. In the black and white phase, parties prefer short-term wins at the expense of the long-term defeat of democracy. Party has become more important than democracy. They will try to manipulate every system within the body of democracy to their advantage, no matter how much it hurts the body's health.

"In the black and white phase, instead of choosing the path of open-minded reason to counter dogma, each party tends to think that to remain competitive they have to match dogma with dogma. Even if they have a lot of common ground on an issue, in the black and white phase, each party will find something to disagree on. They cannot handle compromise; they must have war. As James Madison wrote in Federalist ten, 'So strong is this propensity of mankind to fall into mutual animosities, that where no substantial occasion presents itself, the most frivolous and fanciful distinctions have been sufficient to kindle their unfriendly passions and excite their most violent conflicts.' This is the current state of American politics. If the two sides had no current disagreements, they would create one because they prefer to be at war with one another than try to work together.

"How many times in American history has the black and white thinking of partisan politics caused one side to reject the better idea of the other party just because it was the other party's idea, and, as a result, hurt the American populace either economically or in loss of life? No person is always right and everyone else is always wrong. No party is always right and other parties always wrong, but in the black and white phase, parties cannot accept that.

"All of American democracy's major health problems are caused or influenced by the dogmatic two-party system. The American democracy should deal with its problem of partisan dogma because it would help fix almost every other health problem.

"In the brain, dopamine is an important chemical in reward-motivated behavior. The anticipation of reward increases the release of dopamine, motivating a person to pursue a prize. In the body of a healthy democracy, the greatest prize comes from the pursuit of truth, and reason is the dopamine that is released that causes the democracy to hunger and thirst for nutritious truth.

"Dogma is a drug. Dogma is the intoxicating feeling of close-minded certainty that leads a person or group to think they are always right. They never challenge their own beliefs, resent anyone who dares to challenge their views, and sacrifice the pursuit of objective truth for the sake of protecting their subjective opinion. And those that think differently are always wrong or evil. The free press is the nervous system. When the free press allows the body to take the drug of dogma, dogma blocks the brain's release of reason. When a mind becomes addicted to the drug of dogma, replacing reason's dopamine with Dogma's Dope, the body of a democracy becomes convinced that, instead of wanting the pleasure received by pursuing and discovering truth, it should protect its 'good' feeling of close-minded certainty by absorbing information—no matter how false—that supports its certainty, and excrete information that opposes its views—no matter how true.

"To become addicted to Dogma's Dope, the drug must destroy a person's sense of objective reality. To do this, dogma convinces each addicted citizen within a democracy that they care more about objective truth than anybody else, that they see reality the clearest. Essentially, dogma seeks to carry out the subtle shift in a person's mind from caring about truth to caring only about their *opinion* of the truth.

"Many within both major parties have replaced rigorous intellectual workouts and disciplined diets of nutritious truth with using the drug of dogma. They think Dogma's Dope is a steroid that makes their mental muscles grow big and strong, but it is a hallucinogen that gives them the illusion that they are a stronger person of reason than others, hiding from themselves their own intellectual weaknesses."

Doctor Democracy silently leaned back, giving me the chance to respond.

**The Party before Parties**

After a silent moment of processing everything the doctor said, I asked, "To save the life of American democracy, how do we deal with the addiction to partisan dogma?"

Doctor Democracy pointed in the direction of the Capitol building three miles away and said, "A healthy democracy requires healthy political dialogue. Healthy political dialogue avoids dogma versus dogma interchanges and instead seeks reason with reason conversations. To achieve that and improve the health of your democracy, American political discourse should be taken back to the culture of the party before parties."

I was confused. "I don't understand."

Doctor Democracy sighed and, eminently patient, leaned forward and locked eyes with me. "In the summer of 1787, four years after the end of the Revolutionary War, the colonies sent fifty-five delegates to Philadelphia. I was there. With George Washington serving as the convention's president, each of those fifty-five delegates brought their different ideologies, biases, state loyalties, false beliefs, jealousies and selfish interests into that building in Philadelphia now known as Independence Hall. Among those fifty-five delegates, every political ideology in America today was in some way represented: far left, left-center, centrist, right-center, and the far right.

"In the midst of all those different competing political ideologies at the Constitutional Convention, the delegates brought a common ideal: reason. Most of the delegates, though they each had strong convictions, checked dogma at the door before stepping into the Assembly Room. They brought different ideas onto the same foundation of Enlightenment that held them all intellectually accountable so that they could turn Independence Hall into a laboratory of ideas where they debated all of their different opinions and made mutual compromises to find common ground for the sake of creating a constitution unlike anything the world had ever seen. And, if delegates became dogmatically argumentative, then the even-keeled Washington was there to stymie tempers and maintain an atmosphere of constructive criticism, intellectual diversity, and mutual compromise.

"On the last day of the convention—September 17, 1787—with the Constitution done and about to be voted on, Ben Franklin, the oldest delegate at eighty-one, gave a speech trying to persuade those still dissatisfied with the Constitution to sign it. He was too ill to deliver it himself, so he had a fellow delegate from Pennsylvania, James Wilson, give the speech. In his speech, Franklin said that there were parts of the constitution he disagreed with, but, with more information and further reflection, he might eventually agree with all of it. There had been many times in his long life he had concluded that he was wrong and changed his mind on issues he thought he would never deviate from. He was fallible and often mistaken on even some of his strongest convictions. Franklin thought it was important that the delegates brought all of their different ideologies to the convention to benefit from their shared wisdom, but no one should expect to receive everything they wanted in the Constitution. Everyone should admit they could be wrong and concede that someone else might have a better idea; a willingness to compromise was paramount. For that reason, Franklin thought every delegate should doubt their own infallibility like he did and sign the Constitution.

"Franklin admitted that his worldview, even in old age, was a work in progress. For this reason, Franklin was willing to doubt his own judgment and concede that others might have a better opinion. Through this speech, he immortalized the Constitutional Convention's spirit of reason, intellectual diversity, and principled compromise.

"I think Washington liked Franklin's speech. From his remarks in his Farewell Address, it seems clear that George Washington did not want political parties because he feared that party factions would cause the government to lose the spirit of Ben's words. But, as many precedents as Washington set, his dream of a party-less country was not one that caught on. The Constitution went into effect in 1789. By 1796, two opposing major political parties had been created, monopolizing American politics and establishing the party system of two dominant and mostly dogmatic parties. Then, the different factions began to see those who thought differently as enemies to destroy, instead of allies to work with to find common ground for the common good. Their competition against one another has persisted until the present day, though their names and positions have shifted and changed. If a two-party system similar to the one the United States has had for almost its entire history had existed before and during the Constitutional Convention, the

Constitution probably would have never been formed and the United States would have never been founded.

"In a letter to Thomas Lomax in 1799, Thomas Jefferson wrote, 'The spirit of 1776 is not dead. It has only been slumbering.' Likewise, the spirit of the Constitutional Convention is not dead. American democracy is sick because of its addiction to dogma, but it still has a strong foundation of Enlightenment principles that has helped it to survive for over two centuries. A world-class athlete may stop working out for a year, but the muscles and bones, though having lost some of their strength and endurance, remember what they used to be and what it will take to return to that level of fitness. Likewise, the body of American democracy still has the muscle memory of reason that the Founders established within it. It just needs to get back into the gym. To improve the health of American democracy and one day put itself back near the top of the fittest democracies, the country must recover the spirit of the Constitutional Convention, the spirit of the party before parties—and it can be done."

### The Remedy

I looked out the window. "Okay, I agree. A healthy democracy requires healthy political dialogue, which is dogma free reason-based discourse. So the dogmatic two-party system is the greatest concern for American democracy's health. But the 'party before parties' idea is a political system *without* parties, and I don't think the two-party system is going anywhere. It is too well established. Nor do I think the two parties are going to renounce dogma. And I am not joining either party to try and bring reason into the political discourse from within. It seemed like McCain wanted to try and recover the spirit of the party before parties by wanting Lieberman as his running mate. But I could never pull off something like that because I don't have McCain's fame, his story, his bipartisan respect, or his high place of honor within American society. I am an unknown, a nobody. If it was going to happen from within the current two-party system, then it would take someone like Senator McCain to pull it off."

Doctor Democracy nodded. "Political parties are not going anywhere. And McCain's approach will not work for you. You don't have his clout, his story, his prestige, his authority, his example, his decades of experience, or, maybe most importantly, the nomination for president of one of the two major parties. To try and bring reason into American politics, you will have to find a method outside of the two-party system."

"Do you have any suggestions, any 'remedies,' doctor?"

Doctor Democracy pointed to my bookshelf at my copy of *The Age of Reason*. "In that book Thomas Paine wrote, 'The most formidable weapon against errors of every kind is reason. I have never used any other, and I trust I never shall.' Likewise, if dogma is the disease, reason is the remedy. The only remedy. I think you already have an idea for how to try and help put American democracy through a dogma detox and improve the health of its political dialogue, but you doubt your ability to have a good idea."

I looked down, ashamed. The doctor was right. "Yes, I have an idea, but I think it sounds ridiculous."

"I like ridiculous ideas," Doctor Democracy said. "Look at how 'ridiculous' of an idea the Declaration of Independence and the Constitution seemed at the time, and they have worked out well."

# The Logos Party

I looked up at the chest pocket of the doctor's lab coat. *If I cannot have the confidence to share my ideas with a character I made up, then how weak am I?* "Okay, fine. This is my idea. Though there were no political parties represented at the Constitutional Convention, the fifty-five delegates acted as if they were one party, a party committed to reason, diversity of opinions, and mutual compromise. You said political parties are not the problem. Dogma is the problem. Maybe...maybe a party, united not around dogma but around Enlightenment principles of reason that reflects the atmosphere of the party before parties' spirit at the Constitutional Convention, could help put democracy through a dogma detox and improve the health of its discourse."

Doctor Democracy slapped his thigh and said, "That doesn't sound so ridiculous. I like it. You want to show the country what healthy, reason-based political debates looks like by creating a reason-based party."

Hesitant, I said, "But I don't think it should be a party that is open for membership."

The doctor raised his right eyebrow curiously. "Go on."

I said, "Plato, who I assume is part of you, in his '*Dialogues*' described the theory of 'the forms'. Everything—from a dog, a building, a tree, a human or even love—has a form, or 'nonphysical essence', that is the perfect idealistic version of an object. The form is not real, but is a blueprint that the real version should aspire to be like. Similarly, instead of creating a real political party that can be joined, we could create a fictional reason-based party that could serve as the form of what a party of reason looks like. Then, let America aspire to imitate an idealistic blueprint of how a political party and political discussions should function if it wants American democracy to thrive and be a beacon of reason."

Doctor Democracy leaned back, and rubbed his chin as he pondered my idea. "Not a real party, but only a blueprint. That could help." He leaned forward and looked me in the eye. "You don't think a reason-based party is realistic, do you?"

I looked away. "I have a lot of doubt."

The doctor leaned back. "I think it is a good idea to create it only as a blueprint for America to compare with the real parties. At least it is a good start." He paused. "And yes, Plato is part of Doctor Democracy." The doctor looked down at his watch. "Well, I think you can take the baton and run with it from here. I have an appointment in the Far East that I don't want to be late for—Japan first and then South Korea." The doctor stood and walked to the door.

I also stood. "Wait, how do I create a reason-based party?"

Doctor Democracy looked back, less patient. "I am not going to hold your hand. All you have to do is create a political party that you would want to join. What is your political affiliation?"

Confused, I said, "I don't have one."

The doctor smiled. "There is a name for that, isn't there?"

"Yes, I am an independent."

Doctor Democracy nodded. "Exactly. Create a reason-based party for independent minds."

"That doesn't help," I said, frustrated.

Doctor Democracy put a hand on my shoulder. "You will figure it out. Look how much you have already figured out." The doctor dropped his hand. He turned, looked at the doorknob, and then looked back at me. "Will you open that for me? I am not real, so I cannot do it."

Awkwardly, I reached around him and opened the door.

Doctor Democracy walked outside and down my front porch stairs. I walked outside and stood at the top of the stairs.

Then, as if he had forgotten something, Doctor Democracy stopped, turned to look up at me and said, "One more thing. In your imagination, I am the embodiment of all the great democratic and philosophical minds of history. All of those minds are dead and not here to say that they agree or disagree with all or part of what we just discussed. Most probably would, but some of those great minds of history might not agree that the two-party system's addiction to dogma is American democracy's greatest health concern. So, out of respect for the dead and history, because it is what a person of reason would do, have enough intellectual humility to not claim to speak definitively about what a person of history thought or would think today."

I nodded in agreement.

Doctor Democracy walked down the street. Once he was out of sight, I walked inside, sat at my desk, and did what any good military officer does: I looked at the large problem and broke it down into smaller problems to attack. The first problem I wanted to attack was creating the two most visible parts of any party, or any organization for that matter: the name and the logo.

# Chapter Two

# The Name and the Logo

## The Name

It felt too bold—even pretentious—to call this reason-based party "The Reason Party." Besides, the name "reason" would not have given the party the feel I wanted. I wanted the new party to have a sense of history. Reason is not new, but reason has to be endlessly renewed in new ways, because dogma is an elusive disease that adapts to reason's remedies. So, I looked up the word "reason" in different languages, and it quickly became obvious what the party's name would be.

Ancient Greece introduced the world to reason and democracy. From ancient Greece flows a River of Reason that has run through history to the present moment, though with many obstacles. Greece's intellectual culture was temporarily suppressed throughout the Dark Ages by a thick Dam of Dogma. Then, beginning in the $14^{th}$ century and extending over the course of the next few centuries, ancient Greece's River of Reason broke through the dam. It poured through the Renaissance, the Enlightenment and the Scientific Revolution and continued pushing forward. America's Founding Fathers were then swept up by the River of Reason, renewing reason through writing the Declaration of Independence, the Constitution, and the Bill of Rights. The River of Reason that flows through to today is fed from ancient Greece who introduced the world to philosophy, logic and democracy.[17] *Logos*, ancient Greece's word for reason, seemed like the ideal name to give the party a sense of history.

In his work titled *Discourses*, Aristotle described three methods of persuasion: *ethos, pathos* and *logos. Ethos*, the origin of the word "ethics," is the method of appealing to the authority, experience or character of a speaker to convince an audience that they are a credible source. *Pathos*, the origin of the word "pathetic" (something that causes pity), is the method of convincing an audience by appealing to their emotions through a passionate presentation, usually by invoking sympathy or anger. And *logos*, the origin of the word "logic," is the method of persuading through reason and evidence. All three methods are useful to making an argument, but reason should be prioritized over authority and passion.

## The Logos Logo

From 1999-2007, between ages 15 to 23, I worked part time as a lion and tiger trainer at a big cat reserve in Ohio: The Siberian Tiger Conservation Association. I helped raise cubs, fed the cats, and went into the cage to interact with the animals. I helped maintain safety when the public came to see the cats and get their picture with them. Lions have been a big part of my life, and I wanted the lion to be the symbol of the Logos Party. Democrats have the donkey, Republicans have the elephant, and the Logos Party has the lion of logic.

---

[17] Democracy was born in Ancient Greece. It was reborn in America during the Age of Enlightenment. I could be wrong, but it seems that democracy is born in reason. I wonder if that means democracy dies in dogma.

# The Logos Party

Throughout history, the lion has probably been used as a symbol more than any other animal. Since it was one of the most used symbols, I found it difficult to create an original lion symbol.

Towards the end of the government shutdown, I went for a run from my house to Capitol Hill. I stopped in front of the statue of Ulysses S. Grant to catch my breath. The four lion statues guarding Grant inspired the idea for the Logos Party logo: the red, white and blue lions of logic who roar reason.[18]

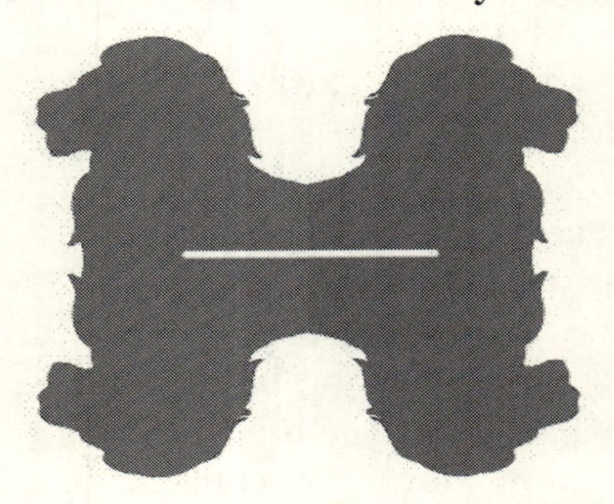

The top two lions of logic guard against dogma in the conscious mind. The bottom two lions of logic guard against dogma in the subconscious. The white line is the divide between the conscious and the subconscious. The lion is largely a nocturnal animal, doing much of its hunting at night. Similarly, the Lions of Logic patrol not only our conscious but the darkness of our subconscious, hunting down and destroying dogma's dogs and certainty's serpents.

The two blue lions of logic guard against dogma from the political left. The two red lions of logic guard against dogma from the political right. All four lions guard the middle area of open-minded reason, intellectual diversity, and principled compromise where progress takes place. The logo reminds party members (called "Logosans") that they should let their passionate lion heart roar, but they should let

---

[18] The logo is black and white here because it saves a lot of money per book. The front cover reflects the actual logo.

their lion of logic mind hold the reins so that they passionately roar reason.

The African lion is an endangered species. But I don't believe the lion of logic is endangered. It feels as if the dogmatic left and the dogmatic right are two different prides of lions (or drove of donkeys and herd of elephants) that appear larger because the members of each do better at roaring together (or hee-hawing and trumpeting together). Meanwhile, lions of logic seem like lions that roam alone in the political wilderness, scattered with no united roar. Lions of logic must roar loudly enough that, scattered throughout the political wilderness, they can hear each other and come together. In this way, independent minds, roaring independently, can also roar as one.

Many might think American politics is not a habitat conducive to lions of logic. But the African lions I worked with in Ohio seemed to adapt well to Ohio winters. Likewise, I believe lions of logic can adapt and thrive in the political environment of the United States. After all, they have before since the country was founded by lions of logic. So American politics is the lion of logic's natural habitat. It is the habitat that has changed, causing them to leave politics. It is time to reintroduce the species to its natural environment.

# Chapter Three

# The Remedy of Reason

The last day of the government shutdown was Friday January 25, 2019. I reported back to work on Monday January 28th. Doctor Democracy said that reason was the remedy to American democracy's health problems. So, I spent February through May trying to answer three questions: *What is reason? How does a person of reason think? What does a reason-based political party look like?*

This chapter and the next tries to answer the first two questions.

## Raise the Rim: The Importance of Standards

One of the military's favorite mantras is "train to standard." This means two things. First, in all facets of the organization, the military tries to set clear standards in order to instill discipline and establish road markers to monitor achievement. Second, standards must be enforced for them to be effective. A standard has little value if it is not enforced.

I believe reason's goal is to help us search for and find truth. In order for reason to achieve this difficult goal, it is necessary to set clear intellectual standards that are enforced in order to instill discipline and measure progress towards the goal of truth. How we search for and determine what we think is truth is determined by our epistemology. Our epistemology is the foundation underneath our worldview or political platforms, the reasons why we believe what we believe and the method we use to form those reasons.

Let me put it this way. The standard height for a basketball rim is ten feet. If we have to lower the rim to be able to dunk, then I don't think we are a legitimate dunker because we cannot dunk on the standard of ten feet. Thousands of people can dunk on a ten-foot rim (I have never been one of them). I consider those people to be legitimate dunkers because they can dunk on the standard. But if the goal is to find the person who can dunk on the highest rim, then the rim must be raised. If the rim is raised to eleven feet, my guess for the number of people in the world who can dunk on that height would be under a thousand. But that standard still isn't strict enough to determine the highest dunker so the rim must be raised again. Raise the rim to twelve feet and my guess is that there are less than ten people on the planet who can dunk on that height. But that standard might still not be high enough. So, raise the rim inch by inch – 12'1, 12'2, 12'3, 12'4, 12'5, 12'6 – until only one person on the planet can jump high enough to dunk on that height. This means we have raised the standard high enough to find the person who can dunk on the highest rim.

Regardless of the subject, that is the same method for finding truth. If there are twenty theories vying to be the correct answer to a question, we have to raise the standard of evidence, the epistemological basketball rim, so high until only one idea can meet the standard—the truth. If there are twenty theories about what shape the earth is—cube, flat, pyramidal, sphere, hexagonal, et cetera—then the standard of evidence has to be raised so high that only the truth, that earth is a sphere, can meet that standard.[19]

I don't think there is a set standard of evidence that can be used to find truth. If we determine that the highest dunker in the world can dunk on a 12'6 rim, but a year later someone steps onto the court who can *also* dunk on a 12'6 rim, then the standard has to once again be raised to determine the person who can dunk on the highest rim. Similarly, if the standard of evidence is currently set high enough that only one theory on a particular subject can meet that standard, but then years, decades, or centuries later a new theory is introduced that can also meet that current standard of evidence, then reason will again raise the epistemological rim to determine the theory that has the best claim to being truth. In other words, a theory that seems to be proven is always, always, always[20] only tentatively the "proven truth." Another theory could always, always, always arise that stakes just as good a claim, if not a better claim, to being the truth.

The history of the theory of gravity, I think, perfectly exemplifies the need to continuously raise the standard of evidence to search for and find truth. In ancient Greece, Aristotle, in his work *On the Heavens,* made one of the earliest attempts to explain gravity by proposing that objects move toward their "natural place." This "natural place" was the center of the Earth, which Aristotle seemed to think was the center of the universe. For about 2,000 years, Aristotle's theory of gravity was the standard epistemological rim height that no other theory could jump as high as. Copernicus and Galileo later debunked the geocentric theory and caused the need for the rim to be raised higher. Then Isaac Newton

---

[19] Technically, the earth is considered to be an oblate spheroid.
[20] Always, always always…ad infinitum.

discovered that the falling motion observed on Earth was the same motion that every object in the universe experienced, holding them in place in relation to each other. He also developed the law of gravity to determine the force of attraction between any two objects with mass. Newton's law of gravity would define mankind's understanding on gravity for more than two centuries.

Then in the early 20th century the rim had to be raised higher when Albert Einstein revolutionized the thinking on gravity through his general theory of relativity, explaining that mass actually bends the fabric of space and time. But general relativity is not compatible with much of quantum physics. So, the rim has been raised again as physicists try to find a comprehensive theory of gravity that can incorporate the general theory of relativity (big scale like planets, solar systems and galaxies) and quantum physics (small scale like atoms, protons and electrons).

At each stage of discovery in physics pertaining to the theory of gravity, the current best theory has only ever been the tentative truth. The epistemological rim is never permanently fixed at a particular height because new theories could always be formed that challenge the credibility of the current best opinion of the truth. But, once set, the rim should never be lowered. If it is going to be moved, it should only be raised. Even when reason finds truth, reason keeps searching and challenging because—as the history of gravity shows us—more truth on an issue can always seem to be found if the rim continues to be raised.

Clarence Darrow, one of the lawyers of the Scopes Monkey Trial, wrote in his memoir *The Story of My Life*, "Chase after the truth like all hell and you'll free yourself, even though you never touch its coat tails." That quote defines reason. Reason sets a high standard of evidence, and then whenever a theory gets close to meeting that standard, the standard is raised. Reason sees no end to the amount of truth that can be pulled out of a subject, no end to the stones that can be turned over. Reason always keeps the standard above what any theory can reach. That way, certainty—which hinders intellectual progress—can never be attained. In other words, if one of the military's favorite mantras is "train to standard," then I believe one of reason's mantras should be "Set the standard beyond certainty's reach."

### Playing on Two Rims

A lot of people consider themselves to be reasonable and someone who cares about finding truth. But the reality is that, in many areas of life, they are a person of dogma who only cares about their *opinion* of the truth. I think there is a big difference between caring about truth and caring only about our opinion of the truth. If we care about truth, then we raise the rim high, creating a difficult standard of evidence that weeds out false ideas—even if they are our own beliefs—leaving us only with the truth. If we care more about our opinion of the truth, then we lower the rim, creating a weak standard of evidence that our unsubstantiated opinions can meet.

This latter person is not open to their mind being changed. They claim certainty, but they don't challenge their own beliefs. They fabricate evidence (knowingly or unknowingly) to support their views, and they resent those who dare to challenge their beliefs. On the other hand, if a person truly cares about truth, they welcome differences of opinion and are open to changing their beliefs if new evidence leads them to conclude that their opinions should be revised. If a party cares about truth, then I think its members would be willing to admit that they could be wrong, challenge their own views, and welcome others challenging their beliefs. If one of their views is false, they want to know so that they can get rid of it and make room for the truth.

People who think they are always right lower the rim to wherever they need it to be to feel that all their views are validated. A person who raises the rim may believe that all their views are true, but they also believe that there are probably a lot of false or weak ideas in their worldview—because history has shown that to be the case, just like Benjamin Franklin expressed in his convention speech. Because they care more about truth than their opinion of the truth, they want the flaws in their worldview exposed. They want to remove the false to make room for the true, even if the truth has not yet been discovered. As Thomas Jefferson wrote, "It is always better to have no ideas than false ones; to believe nothing, than to believe what is wrong."[21]

It took me a while to see the difference between the two. I realized I was a person who often lowered the rim to validate my beliefs instead of raising the rim to search for truth. For example, one of the most important beliefs of my worldview, a belief I held throughout my teens and early twenties, used to be that earth and the universe were less than 10,000 years old. In high school and college, I rejected any evidence or arguments that suggested the universe was billions of years old.

I would lower the epistemological rim to wherever I needed it to be to "confirm" my belief in a young universe. Then I would guard that low rim from

---

[21] Jefferson wrote this line in a letter to the Rev. James Madison on July 19, 1788.

any person who tried to play on it with counter arguments. This way, they could not show me that their views could also dunk on that low rim height or weak standard. Instead, I would raise the rim for counter arguments, creating an unreasonably difficult standard that they could not meet. I did whatever I had to do to protect my opinion of the truth, thinking the whole time that by doing this I cared about truth.

Finally, at age 23, a quote revolutionized my life. It was by a 17th century English historian named Thomas Fuller who supposedly wrote, "Truth fears no trial."[22] I realized that truth does not want to be protected but challenged. Challenging the truth separates it from false ideas. So, I raised the rim to a much higher standard and weighed all the arguments and evidence evenly. As a result, I eventually concluded that the universe was probably billions of years old. But, because my standard of evidence necessary to remove all doubt can never be reached, I am willing to admit that even that belief could be wrong, or at least there is more truth to pull from the claim. Now, every idea I believe to be true can only be tentatively the truth.

Because I have raised the rim by which I measure truth to a standard that can never be met, I believe I have freed my mind because a standard of evidence beyond certainty's reach that can never be met will forever expose the flaws in my own thinking, so I can never again touch certainty's coattails, that feeling of dogma that enslaved my mind and still enslaves millions. I have put a block under my rim so that it can never be lowered, whereas before I used to put a block over my rim so that it could not be raised. If I ever fell prey to feeling certainty again it would

[22] Many people attribute this quote to Fuller, but I couldn't find where he actually wrote it.

mean that I grew intellectually weak, removed the block, and lowered my rim.

## The Canyon of Doubt

Although no theory can ever meet my standard of evidence and be confirmed as truth beyond all doubt, I still believe in many things. I do not need full knowledge before I believe. Picture yourself standing at the edge of the Grand Canyon. You are on the cliff of unbelief. In front of you is the canyon of doubt. On the other side is the cliff of belief and truth. Evidence discovered in favor of a theory can shrink the canyon. I don't think the canyon will ever be erased so that the two cliffs meet, because I don't think it is possible to prove beyond all doubt that something is the truth. There will always be a canyon of doubt, no matter how small.

But if the canyon has been closed substantially by evidence, more than any other current theory, then that theory can be considered the tentative truth; we can allow our bridge of faith to reach across and connect to the cliff of belief. But reason does not forget that faith is a bridge over the canyon of doubt, and not an eraser. That means that if belief requires a half mile wide bridge of faith to get to belief then there must also be a half mile wide canyon of doubt that reason is honest about. Reason understands that faith is a unique resource, the only of its kind, that allows us to move forward to belief and action while maintaining room for doubt.

## Objective v. Relative

Some believe that all truth is relative. But most of our experiences appear to validate that to be false. Wherever we go, things happen regardless of what we believe. There doesn't appear to be any real evidence of things occurring just because we wished really hard that they would. If it did, the world would be chaotic and unpredictable because everyone would be wishing for different things. Everything we do relies upon the idea that there are things which are true independently of us.

Objective reality has a way of forcing itself onto us, no matter what we believe. One of the places we see this happen is in our health. I had cancer in 2005. Once I noticed something might be wrong, I ignored the potential problem for weeks. During those weeks, I lowered my rim so that I could affirm my opinion that nothing serious was wrong. Eventually, as the problem worsened, objective reality forced its way onto me, and I had to raise the rim and go to the doctor.[23]

Some believe that both relative truth and objective truth exists. Personally, I believe there is only objective truth. So, to care about truth is to care about objective truth. I think what people call relative truth is only a person's opinion. Reason does not care about a person's opinion of the truth because a person's opinion has no bearing on whether objective truth is true. Thus, reason cares only about objective truth, the only kind that exists. And if you want to find objective truth then you have to use an objective standard of measurement, a rim raised high beyond certainty's subjective reach.

---

[23] I wonder how many people who believed that all truth is relative are now objectively dead.

Our opinion is itself an objective truth. Our opinion of the truth might be wrong, but the fact that we have an opinion at a moment in time is an objective truth. For example, it is only my opinion of what I think is the best color. But the fact that I have an opinion of what my favorite color is—which is purple—is itself objective. If a year from now my opinion on what is my favorite color changes to green, it is still an objective truth that right now my favorite color is purple.

The difference between reason and dogma is that reason cares about truth, and dogma only cares about its opinion of the truth. Reason raises the rim to find truth. Dogma lowers the rim to affirm its opinion of the truth. Dogma sits back and dictates relative truth (opinion), while reason has to go searching for objective truth. If relative truth exists, all we need is the ability to form an opinion. It is easy to determine our opinion of the truth; it is difficult to determine *the* truth. Dogma lowers the rim and defends its opinion of the truth; reason raises the rim and pursues truth.

## The Two Phases of Reason

### Phase One Reason: Basic Training

Reason's singular goal is to help us search for and find truth. I think reason has two phases in helping us achieve that goal. The first phase is basic training. At basic training, soldiers learn the fundamental skills of soldiering: shooting, staying physically fit (by military standards), land navigation, battle drills, bed making, and other skills. Similarly, the first phase of reason represents the fundamentals of reason, which includes showing us how difficult it is to determine truth, the importance of setting the epistemological standards of evidence high, and how to instill and maintain the intellectual discipline necessary to weed out false theories and prevent dogma and emotional bias.

Most people who go to basic training can make it through basic training. Drill sergeants are tough, but the training is designed to bring soldiers along somewhat at their own pace, giving them a good chance at graduating. Likewise, most people can achieve phase one reason. I think everyone is capable of understanding how difficult it is to determine truth.

### Phase Two Reason: Officer Candidate School

At Officer Candidate School, the goal is to find the best leaders. When I attended Officer Candidate School in January of 2013, my class started with about 240 soldiers. Ten weeks later about 140 soldiers graduated. To help weed out those 100 soldiers, the instructors did things like take away sleep, limit food, and put soldiers in increasingly stressful situations to try and break us. Similarly, phase two reason is the officer candidate school where, after taking us through basic training and showing us how difficult truth is to determine, reason helps us do the hard work of weeding out all the false theories. It demands we find truth by creating and enforcing standards so difficult to meet that only truth can meet them.

Reason wants everybody to realize how difficult it is to find truth. It may take years, decades or centuries of trial and error to find the truth on a subject. Reason wants to find the best truth-seekers. We all can try to weed out false theories to find truth, but reason wants those people who are specialists—

like scientists and historians—who are skilled at finding truth and are willing to devote their life to it. Then the rest of us can benefit from their hard work. For example, we all can realize that it may be difficult to find a cure for a particular disease, but then there are those select few who have the genius and the will to find a cure. And we are all the better for it.

### The REASON Acronym

In order to help explain reason, I created an acronym out of the word reason.

**Reason:** **R**uthless, **E**nergetic, **A**nalytical, **S**trict, **O**bjective, **N**ever-ending

**Ruthless:** Truth is far outnumbered by false ideas trying to convince the world that they are the truth. Because of this, reason must be ruthless to all ideas, mercilessly challenging their credibility.

In the movie *The Terminator*, the Terminator is an emotionless cyborg assassin sent from the future, programmed with one mission: kill Sarah Connor, the future mother of the man who will save humanity from the machines in a post-apocalyptic future. Similarly, reason is Truth's Terminator. Reason is emotionless and unsympathetic, single-mindedly programmed with one mission: get us to truth. To get us to truth, reason is a systematic killing machine, a weapon of mass destruction that destroys all obstacles on the trail to truth, leaving a path of smoldering false ideas. Truth's Terminator does not care about breaking our heart by killing our beliefs that gave us hope and joy. The only hope Truth's Terminator wants to give us is the kind of hope based in reality.

When false ideas see Truth's Terminator coming towards them, they cower in fear. False ideas don't want to be challenged because through testing they are exposed as false. On the other hand, "Truth fears no trial." Truth wants to be challenged because that is how it separates itself from false ideas. Truth welcomes the approach of reason because Truth's Terminator will use all of its weapons to try and destroy it, but will be unable to do so. Then, when the dust settles after Truth's Terminator has rained down all of its fire power onto truth, truth will still be standing triumphant on a pile of dead false theories.

Once Truth's Terminator is programmed with its mission and released in our mind, it is difficult to reverse its course. When Truth's Terminator first entered my mind, it wreaked havoc, leaving a trail of destruction and destroying large portions of my worldview.

I resisted, trying to protect many of my beliefs. Voltaire wrote, "It is difficult to free men of the chains they revere."[24] Even as ruthless reason exposed them as weak, I clung to many of my beliefs. But Truth's Terminator is relentless, and, once in my mind, I could not kick him out.

Someone once said, "The truth will set you free, but first it will make you miserable."[25] That quote defined my life in the first few years after Truth's Terminator was released in my mind. But, as time passed, I embraced the ruthlessness. Now, since I want a worldview full of nothing but the truth, I

---

[24] Voltaire wrote this line in his anonymously published work *Le dîner du comte de Boulainvilliers* (1767).

[25] This quote is often attributed to President Garfield, but it is not found in any of his speeches or letters. The earliest location it appears to be found is in a 1978 Syracuse, New York newspaper article about a treatment program for alcoholics.

rejoice when a false idea in my worldview is destroyed so that truth can rise victoriously to the top.

Reason is unsympathetic to our false beliefs, but reason, in its emotionless way, does seem to care about us more than anyone else, because reason wants to lead us to the most important thing—truth.

I picture reason, Truth's Terminator, being sent back in time to us from a distant future where dogma has been destroyed and humanity lives in an entirely enlightened world. It is here to help us destroy dogma in our present moment. And I picture dogma being sent to us in the present as Certainty's Soldier on a crusade from the distant past: the Dark Ages where dogma reigned supreme. It tries to pull our minds back into the past where the darkness of dogma blocked out the light of logic.

**Energetic:** Reason does not casually pursue truth. Instead, reason chases truth with all its energy, ambition, and passion. As Truth's Terminator, reason is programmed to do nothing but pursue truth with a truth-at-all-costs, single-minded determination. In *Walden*, Henry David Thoreau wrote, "Rather than love, than money, than fame, give me truth." That is a person of reason's mantra.

**Analytical**: Reason is analytical, taking the complexity of an idea and breaking it down into simpler parts to examine it more closely. Reason is detail-oriented, demanding quantifiable precision, and is unwilling to settle for generalized, superficial, or one-sided summaries of an idea. Reason wants to immediately have the truth, but reason is also patient, understanding that pursuing truth can be tedious work.

**Strict**: In order to find truth, reason understands that strict standards of evidence have to be set and followed, a standard beyond certainty's reach. This helps us weed out false ideas and measure progress. But Truth's Terminator does not have a single standard of evidence. Instead, like the epistemological basketball rim that is continuously raised, Truth's Terminator continuously upgrades its weaponry to find and destroy false ideas.

**Objective**: Reason's goal is to get us to truth. The only kind of truth that exists is objective truth; everything else is just opinion. And finding objective truth requires an objective standard. As Truth's Terminator, reason does not allow emotional bias to obstruct the search for truth. Reason does not allow a person to hold their own beliefs—no matter how much they cherish them—to weaker standards of evidence so that they can pass the test. Reason forces a person to challenge their own ideas just as much, if not more, than they challenge opposing views, holding all to the same strict standard.

**Never-ending:** Reason's purpose is to help us search for and find truth. But, even after reason finds truth, it never stops challenging that idea. Reason never concludes that an idea is so well-proven that it should never be challenged again. Reason believes that there could always be more truth pulled from an idea, so reason continues to raise the standard of evidence beyond certainty's reach, challenging it, raising the rim so the standard can never be met.

**Biggest Misconception**

Many people define reason this way: "If you agree with them then you are a person of reason, and if you hold an opposing view then you must be irrational." I think this is maybe the biggest misconception concerning reason. Reason is not about the conclusions we come to, but our method of coming to conclusions. A person's belief could be the truth, but they may not have good reasons for believing that truth. A person could believe the truth that the sky looks blue, but their reason for believing it could be that they think god's eyes are blue. During the day, god's eyes are open, and at night god closes his eyes and that is why it is dark.

A person can have a mind full of truth, and they could even have good reasons for believing in those truths, but they could still not be a person of reason because they are dogmatic about all of those beliefs. Though they believe in truth, they could be claiming that they are *certain* they are right. They never challenge their own beliefs, they resent those who challenge their beliefs, and they do not see their worldview as a work in progress. They have lowered their rim to a level where they can feel certainty, and in so doing have rejected the idea that there is always more truth that can be pulled from a truth.

Also, a person can have a mind full of false beliefs and yet be a person of reason. A person of reason admits they could be wrong, they see their worldview as a work in progress, they challenge their own views, and they welcome others challenging their beliefs. So, even though they have many false beliefs, there is hope that they eventually get to the truth on each issue. As Thomas Jefferson wrote in his first Inaugural Address, "Error of opinion may be tolerated where reason is left free to combat it."

This means that the person of reason who currently has many false beliefs may one day surpass in knowledge the person whose worldview currently consists of more truth, but who is dogmatically unchanging about their views.

**The first two questions answered**

This chapter tries to answer two questions: *What is reason? How does a person of reason think?*

My short answer to the first question is, "Reason is the mind's ability to break down barriers between ignorance and truth." In contrast, dogma is defined as "The mind's ability to erect barriers to protect our opinion of the truth." To break down those barriers, reason must convince a mind that truth is difficult to find and prove. Then, reason raises the standard of evidence beyond certainty's reach so that there is always room for doubt. As a result, no idea is ever proven beyond all doubt, but the truth is still able to rise above all the false ideas vying to be the truth. If the standard of evidence is too low, then false ideas may also be able to meet it.

The answer to the second question is that since they use a standard of evidence that is beyond certainty's reach, a person of reason is intellectually humble, and they admit that they could be either partly or completely wrong on everything they believe. A person of reason could be right on everything, but they are willing to admit that they could be wrong because there is always room for doubt and never room for certainty. Secondly, because there is always room for doubt, a person of reason challenges the credibility of their own beliefs, and they challenge their own views more than they challenge anybody else's beliefs. A person of reason's goal is a worldview that consists of nothing but truth. They understand that there are probably false ideas in their thinking, so they constantly try to expose the false in their own views so they can remove it and make room for truth.

Thirdly, since a person of reason wants help in finding the false in their own worldview, they welcome other people challenging their beliefs. They don't resent their views being challenged. Instead, because they don't trust themselves to find all the false ideas in their own thinking, they appreciate it. Lastly, since they are constantly trying to find the false ideas in their own system of beliefs, a person of reason sees their worldview as a work that is always in progress and their mind is open to being changed.

In short, a person of reason sets the standard of evidence beyond certainty's reach so that there is always room for doubt and never room for certainty. Since there is always room for doubt, they are intellectually humble and admit they could be wrong, challenge their own views, welcome others challenging their beliefs, and see their worldview as a work that is always in progress, so their mind is forever open to being changed.

***

As I finished formulating my opinion of what reason is and how a person of reason thinks, I wondered what country Doctor Democracy was in—maybe Australia, France, or South Africa. I wished for another house call so that he could say whether or not my explanation of reason was adequate before I started creating the Logos Party.

# Chapter Four

# The Rules of Reason

Based on my understanding of reason from the last chapter, I created ten Rules of Reason to serve as the foundation of the Logos Party. The Rules of Reason are not conclusive, but they provide a good understanding of how the Logos Party believes a person of reason thinks. Also listed below are the Doctrines of Dogma, which, principle for principle, are the antithesis of the Rules of Reason.

## The Rules of Reason

1. Science is the most reliable path to truth.
2. Truth wants to be challenged; only false ideas fear doubt.
3. Challenge your own beliefs, and admit you could be wrong.
4. Renounce certainty.
5. Revising your beliefs is okay.
6. Place the burden of proof on yourself.
7. Nothing is sacred.
8. Truth is more important than hope.
9. Faith and doubt are allies.
10. Principled compromise is a reliable path to progress.

## The Doctrines of Dogma

1. Follow science unless it contradicts your views.

2. Truth wants to be protected from doubt.
3. Never challenge your own views or admit you could be wrong.
4. Claim certainty.
5. Never change any of your beliefs.
6. Do not burden yourself with providing objective evidence.
7. The sacred is unchallengeable.
8. Whatever gives you hope is truth.
9. Faith and doubt are enemies.
10. Never compromise.

### 1. Science is the most reliable path to truth.

In his work *The Age of Reason*, the great writer of the Revolutionary War Thomas Paine wrote, "Man cannot make principles; he can only discover them." Likewise, I don't think humans created science. I believe we discovered the method that allowed us to find truth and then called that method "science." Science, more than any other method, constantly raises the epistemological rim, keeping the standard of evidence well out of certainty's reach, in order to filter out false or weak theories and maintain a constant presence of doubt. I think the scientific method is not only the most reliable path to truth, but maybe the only path.

### 2. Truth wants to be challenged; only false ideas fear doubt.

Truth wants to be tested by the toughest epistemological standards because truth cannot be disproven: trying to do so will only strengthen its claim to being truth. Only false ideas fear skepticism because being challenged might expose their falsehood. Truth wants the rim raised high. It wants

Truth's Terminator to try and destroy it. Thomas Paine expressed this idea eloquently when he wrote, "It is error only, and not truth, that shrinks from inquiry."[26]

**3. Challenge your own beliefs and admit you could be wrong.**

Thomas Jefferson wrote, "I was bold in the pursuit of knowledge, never fearing to follow truth and reason to whatever results they led, and bearding every authority which stood in their way."[27] Likewise, a member of the Logos Party, a Logosan, challenges the credibility of their own views just as much as (if not more than) they challenge other people's beliefs, never fearing their beliefs being disproven. Instead, they welcome being refuted because if one of their views is false, they want to know so that they can discard it and make room for truth. Jefferson also wrote, "He who knows best knows how little he knows." Likewise, a Logosan understands the limits of his knowledge and admit that his beliefs could be wrong. This is a sign of intellectual maturity, and it keeps his mind open to finding truth if his current belief on an issue is ever found to be false.

**4. Renounce certainty.**

Since reason sets the standard of evidence beyond certainty's reach, renouncing certainty is fundamental to being a person and party of reason.

---

[26] Paine wrote this line in his 1792 letter titled "Address to the Addressers."

[27] Jefferson wrote this line in a letter to Dr. Thomas Cooper on February 10, 1814.

Voltaire wrote, "Doubt is uncomfortable, but certainty is ridiculous."[28] Throughout history, there have been many ideas that many people felt certain were true but have since been disproven. Centuries from now, many of the beliefs that people feel certain are true today will probably be proven false. So, since history has shown that the feeling of certainty seems like an unreliable gauge for determining truth, the Logos Party renounces the feeling of certainty. The epistemological rim is always higher than what certainty can reach. For the Logos Party, certainty is ridiculous, an intellectual vice that prohibits progress and prevents us from seeing the flaws in our own beliefs. A Logosan wants to see the flaws in their own worldview.

**5. Revising your beliefs is okay.**

The Logos Party believes that it is ignorant to close ourselves off to the possibility of being wrong, because we would be denying ourselves the chance to gain greater knowledge. If we cannot yet be in possession of truth on a particular subject because the truth has not yet been discovered, then we will at least be open-minded and be in possession of wisdom. A Logos Party member believes their worldview could always be better, so their beliefs are always in progress. Because of this, it is not only okay to revise our beliefs, it is expected.

**6. Place the burden of proof on yourself.**

A Logosan does not wait for someone else to put the burden of proof on them. He puts it on himself. They not only expect other people to test their views by a high standard and provide credible

---

[28] Voltaire wrote this line in a letter to Frederick William, Prince of Prussia on November 28, 1770.

evidence, but also hold themselves to the same standard. They set the rim just as high for their own beliefs as they do for others, maybe higher. A Logosan does not have a double standard, raising the rim to test other people's views, while lowering the rim when testing their own.

**7. Nothing is sacred.**

Everything—from religions, to political ideologies, to cultures, sports teams, et cetera— is considered sacred to somebody. If something was not challenged because someone else considered it sacred, nothing would ever be challenged. It is fitting that the word "sacred" is so similar to the word "scared," because a person who calls their beliefs sacred is probably afraid their sacred beliefs could be wrong. They hope the label of "sacredness" will protect that belief from being challenged and exposed. In the Logos Party, the idea closest to being sacred is that nothing is sacred, therefore everything should be relentlessly challenged, especially our own views.

**8. Truth is more important than hope.**

Hope is necessary for the world, but truth is more important to the world because truth is what fixes problems. Hope is not confirmation of truth. Something does not have to be true for it to give hope, nor does it have to inspire hope in order to be true. Often, a painful truth can cause hopelessness. The Logos Party tries to first find truth, even if painful, and then figures out how to find hope within the context of reality.

**9. Faith and doubt are allies.**

In the search for truth, faith and doubt are on the same team. Doubt helps us challenge an idea's credibility and understand what little we know. Faith does not erase doubt. Instead, it bridges the canyon of doubt, helping us step out into uncertainty in search of finding answers to the questions doubt raises. In other words: doubt shows us the limits of our knowledge, and faith (with reason) helps take us beyond those limits. The common enemy of both faith and doubt is dogma.

**10. Principled compromise is a reliable path to progress.**

No person or party has a monopoly on good ideas. If we have any chance at seeing the whole picture and collectively moving forward in progress, then we require other people's viewpoints, especially those different than our own. The culture of compromise within the Logos Party fosters within members a willingness to listen to new ideas, try to understand opposing views, and collaborate toward a shared goal as long as all are willing to make principled compromises. As President Ford said, "Compromise is the oil that makes governments go."

## Constructive Criticism

The only type of criticism acceptable by Logosans—either inwardly toward one another or outwardly toward non-members—is constructive criticism. Constructive criticism is defined as, "the process of offering valid and well-reasoned opinions about the work of others, usually involving both positive and negative comments, in a friendly manner rather than an oppositional one, with the goal of improving a person instead of degrading them."[29]

---

[29] I found this on the website www.definitions.net.

Constructive criticism is not a Rule of Reason, but is the atmosphere in which the Rules of Reason thrive.

**The Tournament of Truth**

Every March, teams are put into a bracket known as the NCAA basketball tournament. Through tough competition, these teams are whittled down to one who is crowned the champion. Likewise, all theories vying to be the truth on a subject get placed into a bracket in the "Tournament of Truth." Then, through tough competition guided by ruthless reason, theories eliminate one another until only one survives—the truth. On the other hand, when a Tournament of Truth is run by the Doctrines of Dogma, the epistemological standards of competition are so weak that truth cannot defeat false ideas because every theory can meet dogma's standards of evidence. If you care about truth, raise the rim beyond certainty and dogma's reach by following the Rules of Reason.

## Chapter Five

## A New Party Paradigm

At the beginning of chapter two I mentioned three questions I thought I had to answer to create the Logos Party. The first was *what is reason?* The second question was *how does a person of reason think?* In the last two chapters I tried to answer those questions. The third question was, *what does a reason-based political party look like?* The rest of the book tries to answer that question.

Reason sets the standard of evidence beyond certainty's reach so that there is always room for doubt, which causes a person of reason to be intellectually humble and admit they could be wrong, challenge their own views, welcome the skepticism of others, and treat their worldview as a work that is always in progress so that their mind is open to being changed. *So, in light of that explanation of reason, how does a political party have to be formed to create a culture in which its members can live out being people of reason?*

***

A person's political worldview consists of their platform views—their belief on topics like national security, the economy, foreign policy and education—and the foundation or epistemology that platform is built on. The uniqueness of the Logos Party is that it places greater importance on the foundation, the method of how a person determines truth and forms their political beliefs, instead of the political beliefs themselves. For the Logos Party, this foundation is described by the Rules of Reason. But, after creating this foundation, I struggled with what the party's platform of political beliefs it endorses that are built on top of that foundation should be.

I didn't want the party's platform to be entirely my views. My goal is not to have everyone align with my political beliefs; that would prohibit intellectual diversity and make the Logos Party look too much like a dogmatic party whose leaders expect all members to fall in line ideologically with the party's officially endorsed platform. If George Washington had begun the Constitutional Convention by explaining his political platform and what he expected the constitution to look like, that would have probably hurt the conventions goal of intellectual diversity because many delegates may have felt compelled to fall in line with Washington's views.

I have identified as an independent since 2008 because I could never bring myself to join a political party that expected me to sacrifice open-mindedness and reason in order to dogmatically believe in its entire platform. Thomas Jefferson wrote:

> "I never submitted the whole system of my opinions to the creed of any party of men whatever, in religion, in philosophy, in politics, or in anything else, where I was capable of thinking for myself. Such an addiction is the last degradation of a free and moral agent."[30]

Like Jefferson, I never could have submitted the whole system of my opinions to the creed of any

[30] Jefferson wrote this line in a letter to Francis Hopkinson on March 13, 1789.

party, and I want the Logos Party to have no hint of being the type of party that I refuse to join. I want to avoid the risk of creating a mob mentality that causes people to be uncritical of their own group and only critical of those who think differently. I want the Logos Party to be built to resist the mob mentality.

Besides, my current political platform consists of views from the left, right, and middle, and that might not have broad appeal. Third parties are often niche parties with small audiences because of how narrow their political platform is. Reason should have broad appeal. Also, as I continue challenging my own views, my current platform is subject to change, which it has done repeatedly over the years. So, if the Logos Party is my platform, it would have to be constantly revised.

Since I don't want the Logos Party's platform to be my platform for fear of prohibiting intellectual diversity, I began to study what the majority of independents believed politically. If I could find a general consensus, perhaps I could build the party's platform around those views. But what I found was that, though there was a strong and widespread desire in the United States for a third party because the two-party system does not adequately represent America's political diversity, there is no consensus as to what a major third party should look like. Some independents wanted a party further right than Republicans, some wanted one further left than Democrats, and others wanted a centrist party. It seemed as though, there had to be at least five major political parties: far-left, left-center, centrist, right-center, and far-right. I concluded that if I gave the Logos Party a platform that leaned any of those directions, I would be sacrificing the potential for broad appeal, excluding many independents and prohibiting intellectual diversity.

I wanted members of the Logos Party to feel free to think for themselves, but I feared that any party platform would hurt that goal. So, for weeks, from the second half of February through the first part of March, I struggled with two questions:

1. H*ow could the Logos Party have a political platform and maintain broad appeal without in anyway prohibiting intellectual diversity?*
2. *How does the Logos Party have an official platform of policies it endorses while at the same time keeping the primary focus on the party's foundation, the idea that the method of how we form beliefs is more important than our beliefs?*

***

Beginning in the summer of 2018, I ended almost every work week with a run around the Washington Mall. Starting at Franklin Square, I would run down 13th Street, turn left on H Street, right on 10th Street, past Ford Theater and FBI headquarters, left on Pennsylvania Avenue, up and around the Capitol Building, past the Air and Space Museum and Smithsonian Castle, past the Washington Monument to the Lincoln Memorial, up and down the Lincoln stairs a few times, along the reflection pool and around the WWII Memorial, left on 17th Street, right on Pennsylvania Avenue, walk past the White House through Lafayette Square, and then jog back to Franklin Square.

Starting in March of 2019, I began expanding the run. After going around the Capitol Building, instead of running past the Washington Monument to the Lincoln Memorial, I would turn left on Raoul Wallenberg Plaza and run past the Holocaust Museum to my favorite Washington D.C. memorial, the Jefferson Memorial.

That first time I ran to the Jefferson Memorial, I stood in the memorial and read the quotes etched on the walls. One leapt out to me that day more than the rest:

> "I am not an advocate for frequent changes in laws and constitutions, but laws and institutions must go hand in hand with the progress of the human mind. As that becomes more developed, more enlightened, as new discoveries are made, new truths discovered and manners and opinions change, with the change of circumstances, institutions must advance also to keep pace with the times."

I thought this Jefferson quote captured the Logos Party idea that a person's epistemological standards should be raised beyond certainty's reach so that our worldview is forever a work in progress. Each Logosan should regularly reexamine and potentially modify their views in light of new evidence and an ever-changing culture so that their beliefs can, as Jefferson wrote, "go hand in hand with the progress of the human mind" and "keep pace with the times."

Standing there in the Jefferson Memorial, I realized that even though I was trying to create a political party that looked differently than any other party, I was still stuck in current political thinking. I still believed that a political party had to have an official platform, an official stance on foreign policy, the economy, social issues, and national security.

Instead, standing there in the Jefferson Memorial, I concluded that to be a foundation-focused party of reason that captures the spirit of the Constitutional Convention, it should not have a platform, official or unofficial. This would allow each party member to think independently and feel comfortable changing their platform views in light of new information they encounter. This would also create a party that is focused on moving forward "hand in hand with the progress of the human mind" and "advancing to keep pace with the times."

Partisan dogma usually arose from having a party platform that all members were expected to believe in, a set of policy views on the economy, foreign policy, social issues, and national security that party members could tribalistically rally around. I concluded that—in order to help eliminate partisan dogma and promote intellectual diversity—a reason-based party should have a standard of reason that unites all members, but no platform that unites them.

Doctor Democracy said I should create the political party I would want to belong to. I finally realized that the party I would want to belong to would not endorse a particular platform that all members are expected to believe in completely, or at all, because that is generally the source of dogma. Instead, the party I would want to join endorses only a standard of reason, which:

1. *fosters a culture of intellectual diversity* that allows in opinions across the full political spectrum. As Jefferson wrote, "Intellectual diversity leads to enquiry, and enquiry to truth."

2. *holds all members intellectually accountable*, mandating that each member check dogma at the door by raising their standard of evidence beyond

> certainty's reach so that they can enter the party onto a shared foundation of reason. As a result, each member should admit they could be wrong, challenge their own views, welcome others challenging their beliefs, and see their worldview as a work that is always in progress.

I think it is safe to say that we all want to belong to a group of like-minded people. Many want to belong to a group of like-minded people on platform issues. I want to belong to a group of like-minded people on the foundation of reason, which creates on top of it a culture of intellectual diversity open to all political leanings so that it does not affirm my platform beliefs, but challenges them. That is the Logos Party.

Finally finding a restless peace about what the Logos Party should look like, I left the Jefferson Memorial and continued my run.

***

That evening after my first Jefferson Memorial run, I sat down at my desk and began writing out why I think a reason-based party with no official platform might actually care more about progress on platform issues like national security and the economy than a platform-focused party like what America is used to. In other words, I think a reason-based party that has no party platform creates stronger individual platforms among party members.

First, the Logos Party does not want to give its members an endorsed platform because doing so may unintentionally obstruct its members from evaluating and modifying their own views because they may feel obligated to fall in line with that endorsed platform, even if they believe something different.

Secondly, a platform-focused party claims to provide the best answers on all policy issues. The Logos Party with no official platform does not claim to provide the best answers. Instead, it claims to provide the decision-making framework for eventually finding all the best answers. Building on reason will lead members to good platforms. But if a member's beliefs are not as good as they could be (which they never are) then the decision-making process of ruthless reason is a self-correcting method that assures never-ending progress.

The Logos Party has a culture of reason-based intellectual diversity because political circumstances are always evolving. This means that one political leaning might offer the best option for one situation, while a different political leaning may offer a better option in a different situation. In order to find the best option for a given situation, a culture of reason and intellectual diversity is needed to determine the best option for that given moment. A reason-based party that welcomes all political platforms will benefit from the joint wisdom of different perspectives and provide the best atmosphere for this kind of progress. Platform-focused parties usually prohibit intellectual diversity because they typically want all members to believe in the same ideas.

Platform-based parties believe the political platform is more important than what the platform is built on. The Logos Party believes the foundation is more important than the platform itself. Dogmatic platform-focused parties sometimes prefer the short-term victory of their party winning at the expense of the long-term defeat of democracy. The Logos Party prefers the short-term "defeat" of compromise for the sake of long-term progress and health of democracy.

Dogmatic platform-based parties care more about their opinion of the truth and will lower the rim to wherever they need it to be to feel that their views are validated. They will create evidence and arguments to support their platform. The Logos Party cares more about truth; it keeps the rim raised high so that false ideas are weeded out, even if that means their views become the casualties.

The Logos Party cares far more about truth than any member's opinion, a party focused more on the quality of the decision-making process; a party focused more on how people think instead of on *what* they think.

President John F. Kennedy said, "Too often we enjoy the comfort of opinion without the discomfort of thought."[31] Leaders of platform-focused parties think they are providing a service to their members by supplying ready-made beliefs on every policy issue, while what they are really doing (intentionally or otherwise) is preventing their members from experiencing the "discomfort of thought," so that members can instead enjoy the comfortable feeling of party opinion. The Logos Party wants its members to experience the "discomfort of thought" that comes through regularly challenging the credibility of their own beliefs. The Logos Party does not want to affirm a member's views, but rather challenge them.

Platform-focused parties are like basic training where the party leaders are drill sergeants who teach party members what to think. A reason-based party is like officer candidate school where instructors empower party members by teaching them how to

---

[31] JFK said this line in a commencement speech he delivered at Yale University on June 11, 1962.

think. As Thomas Paine wrote in *The Rights of Man*, "Reason obeys itself; and ignorance submits to whatever is dictated to it."

***

The two major dogmatic parties often act as if they have always endorsed the platform they currently support. But if you look over the course of the history of both the Republican and Democratic Party you see that both parties' "official" platforms or political leanings have changed many times in fundamental ways. In many ways, the two major parties have gradually reversed positions on many issues.

Founded around 1828 by supporters of Andrew Jackson, the Democratic Party initially supported limited government, a strong system of federalism and state sovereignty, and they were opposed to the abolition of slavery. The Republican Party was founded in the 1850s and, led by the progressive Lincoln, supported a strong federal government, civil rights, more spending on education, and more open immigration. So, throughout the Civil War and the rest of the 19th century, the Democrats were the conservative party and Republicans were the liberal party.

Theodore Roosevelt, president from 1901 to 1909, was a liberal Republican who wanted a "Square Deal" for working families, which sounded very socialistic. He broke up monopolies, championed food and drug regulations, created national parks, and cared more about the environment than any other president. Those ideas now seem to be championed more by Democrats. The Republican Teddy Roosevelt might have been the most progressive president in history. Roosevelt's successor, President Taft, began pulling the Republican Party to the right. Teddy, thinking Taft was pulling the country too far right, challenged Taft for the Republican nomination in 1912. When Teddy lost, this established the Republican Party on its new conservative course.

Roosevelt created a new progressive party called the Bull-Moose Party, which wanted universal medical care, pensions, an 8-hour workday, and minimum wage for women. The Democratic Party began breaking from its conservative roots when, in 1896, it nominated the liberal William Jennings Bryan for president. After Teddy and Bryan, the Republican Party gradually became more conservative, and Democrats more liberal.

In the 1930s, Teddy's nephew, FDR, implemented the "New Deal," which established widespread progressive reform. In the 1950s, Republican President Eisenhower once had a graduated tax system in which the highest rate for the wealthiest was at ninety percent. Now, Republicans seem to be the party of tax breaks for the rich. In the 1960s, President Johnson's "Great Society" furthered the progressive agenda, more greatly establishing Democrats as the liberal party. Then, in the late 70s and throughout the 80s, President Reagan took the Republican Party further right. In the 21st century, the Tea Party arose, trying to take the Republican Party even further right. And the Democratic Party has continued establishing itself as the left-leaning liberal party.

So, for good or bad, the platforms of the two major parties have changed in major and fundamental ways over the course of their histories. The left-leaning Democrats and the right-leaning Republicans may try to forget this, but change has forced its way into both parties, reversing their policy stances on many issues over the course of their history.

Both dogmatic parties dislike each other for their political leanings, blinding themselves to history which says the platforms of both parties have at some time in their history leaned in every political direction: far-left, left-center, centrist, right-center, and far right. At any given moment, each dogmatic party may be close-minded, but, over the course of time, the history of both parties reflect political diversity. The Logos Party, seeing no political leaning as inherently wrong, reflects that intellectual diversity in real time. Though their histories reflect change within their platforms, the two major parties resist change; the Logos Party embraces changing platforms, as long as these changes are inspired by reason.

America has only known a platform-focused two-party system, and that system is increasingly dominated by partisan dogma. Maybe it is time to give a chance to a reason-based culture that actually has the potential of bringing people of different opinions together on the same foundation of reason that guides them all.

## The Three-tiered Paradigm

To simplify the difference between dogmatic platform-focused and reason-based parties, I created the Logos Party's three-tiered paradigm: the foundation, the pillars and the platform. The foundation, the party's method of determining truth (epistemology), are the Rules of Reason.

On top of the Rules of Reason are the Pillars of Progress: wisdom, humility, logic, and passion.[32] A

[32] The pillars can be viewed as a simplified and more memorable version of the Rules of Reason.

member of the Logos Party shows wisdom by understanding the limits of their knowledge. As Benjamin Franklin wrote, “The doorstep to the temple

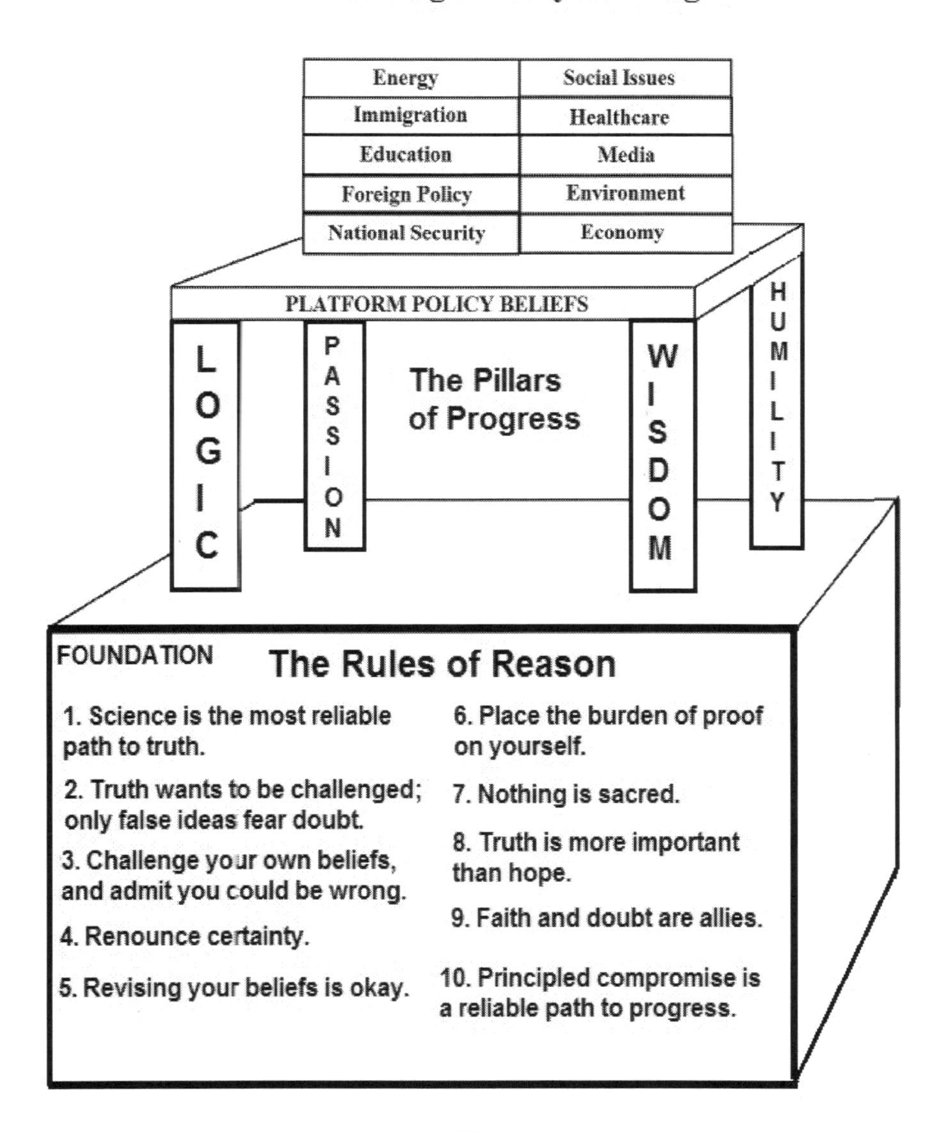

of wisdom is a knowledge of our own ignorance."[33] I don't think a person is ignorant for not having a lot of information stored in their head. I think a person is ignorant if they don't realize the limits of their knowledge.

We all have a sphere of competence. It does not matter as much how broad our sphere of competence is. What is more important is that we understand the limits of our sphere of competence and don't try to go outside of it and claim knowledge that we have no credibility claiming. We should seek to expand our sphere of competence, but we should always stay within our sphere. Then, a person of reason is humble enough to publicly admit those limits. They then use the method of logic, which helps take them beyond those limits and gain greater knowledge. Lastly, a Logosan should be passionate, but they let reason guide their passion. As Benjamin Franklin wrote, "If passion drives you, let reason hold the reigns."[34]

On top of the Pillars of Progress, each Logos Party member builds their personal platform of political beliefs: their views on issues like the economy, national security, foreign policy, the environment, energy, education, and social issues. Each party member is encouraged to promote their personal views. But each member understands that their platform beliefs are held accountable by the Rules of Reason and the Pillars of Progress. This means each member is humble enough to admit they could be wrong, they challenge their own views, they want the world to challenge their beliefs, and they see their worldview as a work forever in progress.

The Logos Party has no platform of policies it endorses, and it is not allowed to have an official

---

[33] Franklin wrote this line in *Poor Richard's Almanac.*

[34] Franklin also wrote this line in *Poor Farmer's Almanac.*

stance on any platform issue. The party promotes only the rules and the pillars. That means that when promoting their personal platform beliefs, a Logosan speaks only on behalf of themselves. Members can speak on behalf of the Logos Party when promoting the Rules of Reason and the Pillars of Progress.

***

Full-time soldiers often have to wake up early and workout with their unit. These workouts are often in unison, so every soldier has to do the same exercises instead of doing a workout tailored specifically to their fitness level. But these group workouts help build unit cohesion, camaraderie, and discipline. Then, in the evening, soldiers who felt the morning workout was not adequate will go to the gym and do their own workout, one better suited to their fitness needs.

That is similar to how I envision the Logos Party. Logosans workout together in unison united around the same strict standard of reason. On this shared foundation of reason is forged a culture of intellectual diversity made up of different platforms, where every member challenge their own beliefs and welcomes other members challenging their views. Each member can build their unique platform of policy beliefs, thus keeping their independent mind. So, within the Logos Party, members can roar together and roar independently at the same time.

In other words, after the morning workout where the whole party works out together using the same fitness regimen of reason, Logosans then workout on their own to form their own political beliefs. Members may work out with others around shared policy concerns, but even these small workout groups hold themselves to the same strict standard of reason to avoid creating mob mentalities within the party.

### Authoritarian Dogma v. Democratic Reason

One of my favorite books, George Orwell's *1984,* offers one of literature's best examples of authoritarian dogma. *1984* opens with the main character, Winston Smith, committing an act of rebellion against the ruling party of Oceania, INGSOC (English Socialist Party)—a regime that seeks to control every aspect of its people's lives, even their thoughts—by opening a journal and, for the first time, writing down his own thoughts. [35]

INGSOC and its leader, Big Brother, are authoritarians that only care about their opinion of the truth, not truth itself (unless the truth happen to support their agenda). Since INGSOC seeks to control every aspect of the people of Oceania's lives, the regime is opposed to the idea of objective reality because then they would have to admit that there is a standard outside of themselves, which would mean they could be wrong. For INGSOC, that is unacceptable.

To control the public's perception of reality, INGSOC has an institution called The Ministry of Truth—who Winston works for—whose job is to continuously revise all news articles and past broadcasts so that history always appears to support

[35] The day of that first journal entry was April 4, 1984. I was born the day before on April 3, 1984. For me, it is symbolic that I was born the day before the opening of Orwell's novel because the regime of INGSOC is the epitome of almost everything the Logos Party stands against. I like to think that maybe on the day I was born Winston Smith was struggling over whether or not to cross his Rubicon River and rebel.

the regimes current narrative on the economy and world events. When a government can control the people's perception of reality to that extent, the ruling party never has to admit that they could be or have been wrong. They can maintain a perception of infallibility in the eyes of the citizenry. When a regime has that level of control, there is no epistemological standards of evidence outside of themselves. They are the standard, and whatever they say is "truth".

INGSOC is a government run by dogma, only caring about its opinion of the truth and not truth, which requires the people to remain ignorant and afraid of speaking out. When a single-party government is the standard of truth, they might pretend to believe in objective reality and even promote the idea of objective truth, while always changing the narrative of reality to whatever they want. Some of history's most notable examples of "Big Brothers" who were able to, for a time, exert this level of control over the people's perception of reality were Hitler, Stalin, Kim Jung-un, and Mao Zedong.

In a multi-party democratic system, it is more difficult to exert the same level of control over the citizenry's perception of reality. In a healthy democracy governed by reason, no party should want to exert that level of control over the people's perception of reality. Instead, every party wants the people to be educated, well-informed and critical thinkers. The media and the political parties would maintain a level of separation so the media could act as an unbiased check on all of government.

In an unhealthy democracy ruled by a dogmatic, multi-party system, controlling the people's perception of reality is easier. Each party has media outlets with wide audiences that support them. They are able to create echo chambers in which they can exert some level of control over their followers' perception of reality.

Authoritarian regimes like INGSOC or the Nazi Party have no legitimate competitors because other parties are not allowed. They often describe a constant enemy in some far-off country, real or imagined, that they use to rally their people's hatred around. This is used to legitimize the need for them to stay in power because they are "needed" to protect the people from that threat. In an unhealthy dogmatic multi-party democracy, instead of using some far-off enemy to rally their follower's hatred and fear against (though they may use this as well), each party will often use the other party as the enemy. Media outlets and social media accounts loyal to them are committed to denigrating the other party. In this kind of democracy, each party serves as an authoritarian competing for power instead of working together in a culture of intellectual diversity that sees one another as allies.

In an authoritarian, dogmatic party like INGSOC, the goal is power for the sake of power. In a healthy democracy, each party wants power, but they want that power for the sake of using reason to pursue truth and further the progress of the whole country.

This does not mean that dogmatic, authoritarian regimes never pursue truth. Nazis regularly used reason to pursue truth when it came to weaponry, raising the epistemological standards high so that they were always producing greater guns, artillery, and bombs, but those weapons were used to defend a dogmatic ideology. Even in propaganda, Nazi's pursued truth: the truth of how to create better propaganda and push their diabolical ideas. They pursued truth only to the extent that those objective truths helped them promote their dogmatic opinion of the truth on their core platform beliefs. In a healthy democracy, every political group pursues truth in every area, not just when it promotes their dogma.

A person or regime that cares only about their opinion of the truth will act as though they created the world. It is a small globe that they control, and they can make spin at will. They can dictate what it looks like and they stand over it like a satellite, sending down messages to the people on earth: "This is what reality looks like." Meanwhile, the leader who is governed by reason cares about truth; they understand that they do not control reality. Therefore, they live as if the planet is far bigger than they are, and their goal is to look up at the sky, receive information from the satellites that orbit earth, and share information about reality so we can piece together a better picture of the world in which we live. They are honest, admitting that we will always only see in part, and we will each spend our whole life trying to put the puzzle of reality together a piece at a time. Dogma thinks it has the whole puzzle put together because it controls reality.

Dogmatic leaders tell the citizenry what the world looks like, while leaders of a healthy democracy help the citizenry discover what the world objectively looks like. Dogma stands outside of reality and tries to control the citizenry's perception of reality. Reason lives within reality and tries to help others and themselves understand it.

John Adams wrote, "Facts are stubborn things; and whatever may be our wishes, our inclinations, or the dictates of our passions, they cannot alter the state of facts and evidence."[36] That is the mindset of a person who believes in an objective reality and standard of evidence that everyone is held

---

[36] Adams said this line in his defense of the British soldiers on trial for the Boston Massacre in 1770.

accountable to. I believe, and I think John Adams believed, that the health of a democracy depends in large part on a widespread belief among both the government and the electorate in objective reality.

Though citizens may differ on what they think objective reality might be, they at least believe in a reality that they are all held accountable to, a truth outside of themselves that is true whether they believe in it or not. This acknowledgement creates within a person enough intellectual humility to admit they could be wrong, which in turn makes them more willing to work together alongside people they disagree with. After all, they are all pursuing the same truth and see their worldview as a work in progress.

As a people's hunger for objective reality and nutritious truth declines—as they lower the epistemological rim—so also declines every system within the body of a democracy. Objective truth is the glue that holds a healthy democracy together, and when a democracy allows party dogma to dominate, the sense of objective reality is lost, the glue weakens, and the democratic government begins to fall apart.

When dogmatic authoritarianism wants to destroy other democracies, they try to destroy within that democracy's electorate a sense of objective reality and a distrust in the political systems. Authoritarians need democracy to look weak, and so create infighting within its parties. In this way, the different parties kill democracy from within, instead of working together to fight the outer threat of authoritarian dogma.

***

As I finished creating the three-tiered paradigm and explaining the benefits of a foundation-focused party over a platform-focused party, I wondered where in the world Doctor Democracy currently was, and I wished for another house call to check my work.

# Chapter Six

# The River of Reason Pledge

When deciding how a person joins the Logos Party, I had two criteria: first, it had to be a simple and symbolic act that is easy to perform; and second, it had to provide a method of holding a member intellectually accountable. I decided that the "River of Reason Pledge" accomplished both.

Besides flowing from ancient Athens to the present, the River of Reason also runs through the mind of every enlightened person. Like a raging river that never stops flowing, a mind with reason flowing through it never stops challenging every idea, even ideas that appear to be convincingly confirmed as truth.

Every idea vying to be the truth travels along Theory Trail up to the river. Then, each theory tries to swim across to be confirmed as truth. If the theory makes it across the river, it is the truth. If a theory is the truth, but not yet proven, then it can tread in the river, but it cannot swim across. If it is not the truth, then it is eventually washed downriver over False Theory Falls.

Like a river trying to cleanse itself of pollutants, the River of Reason is constantly cleansing the mind of dogma and false ideas. In contrast to the cleansing powers of the River of Reason, a mind controlled by dogma is like a stagnant polluted lake that uses the Dam of Dogma to trap in bad information. It is unable to cleanse itself because there is no movement, no continuous challenging of ideas, especially one's own.

If a theory makes it across the river and is confirmed as truth, it can grab the riverbank, but it is not allowed to pull itself out of the river. Lions of logic patrol the riverbank, ensuring no truth climbs out. This way, truth forever feels the resistance of the river, allowing more insight to always be pulled from that truth.

To become a Logosan, a Logos Party member, you raise your right hand and recite the River of Reason Pledge.

**THE RIVER OF REASON PLEDGE**

I, (your name), pledge that I will forever allow the River of Reason to flow through my mind and never block the river with a Dam of Dogma. If any of my beliefs are untrue, no matter how painful the loss, I want them washed over False Theory Falls and out of my mind.

As a member of the Logos Party, my platform will be built on the Rules of Reason and the Pillars of Progress. I will have the courage to expose dogma in other members and myself, and humble enough to listen if others find dogma in me.

If the Logos Party was open for membership, you would have to record yourself taking the pledge and then submit the video on the party website to verify that you took it.

By taking the River of Reason Pledge, you are declaring that you are trying to be a person of reason. According to the Logos Party, that means you believe your political platform should be held to a ruthless standard of evidence that is beyond certainty's reach so that there is always room for doubt, a standard that demands you admit your beliefs could be wrong, that you challenge the credibility of all of your beliefs and others', that you welcome others challenging your views; and, just like 81-year-old Ben Franklin, that you see your worldview as a work that is forever in progress. By taking this pledge, you are declaring that you set your epistemological rim high to help you weed out false ideas and hold yourself intellectually accountable.

You are declaring that the foundation of *how* we think is more important than our platforms and *what* we think. Our method of decision-making is more important than the decisions we make. Our process of how we pursue truth is more important than what we conclude as truth. You are a lifelong learner who holds yourself to a standard of evidence so high that it regularly exposes flaws in your own thinking. You realize that a person of reason is someone who stands up for what they believe in, but a person of reason also stands up to their own beliefs.

By taking the River of Reason Pledge, you agree that, instead of condemning each other for having different beliefs, no matter how many different paths and directions in life we come from, the goal is for all of us to be traveling toward the same destination of truth. You appreciate your worldview being challenged and flaws in your views exposed so that progress can be made.

By taking the pledge, you are admitting that you do not want to belong to a party that affirms your beliefs, but instead a party that challenges your views. You want to belong to a group of diverse views where cordial disagreement is encouraged, especially if done through constructive criticism and not done in a condescending or arrogant way.

By taking the River of Reason Pledge, you are declaring that you fear surrounding yourself with people who think like you on every issue because that is a breeding ground for dogma and the mob mentality. You value being part of a group that cultivates intellectual diversity. You do not consider another person an enemy because they have views different from yours, but instead you see them as allies because, as Thomas Jefferson wrote, "Diversity of opinions lead to enquiry, and enquiry to truth."

By taking the pledge, you are formally declaring war on dogma. You believe dogma is the enemy, and not the person whose mind is being controlled by dogma.

***

Since we all have intellectual lapses, a Logosan may temporarily display dogmatic tendencies. Reason is a standard that even the most rational person at times fails to meet. But, if we hold ourselves accountable to a clear and strict standard of reason, then it will prick our conscience and demand we tear down the dam and practice intellectual humility.[37]

[37] If a member prolongs in dogma and, once confronted about it, refuses to tear down the dam in their mind and raise the standard of evidence beyond certainty's reach, their Logosan membership will be revoked. Anyone who joins the Logos Party can, at any time, renounce the party and leave.

## Chapter Seven

## Founder's Platform

Some are so used to platform-based parties that when they hear of a party that doesn't endorse a specific platform, they think that party doesn't stand for anything. On the contrary, I believe a foundation-focused party that doesn't have a set platform of policies it endorses stands far more strongly for progress than dogmatic platform-based parties.

But, to show the full extent of how a reason-based party contrasts with and is better for progress than a platform-based party, and to prove that I *do* stand strongly on political issues, I thought it was important to explain part of my personal platform, which I build on top of the rules and the pillars.

As discussed earlier, if George Washington had opened the Constitutional Convention by explaining his platform and what he expected to be included in the Constitution, he may have hurt the climate of intellectual diversity because some delegates may have been persuaded to fall in line with his beliefs. That is not my intention in this chapter. If the Logos Party was open for membership, I would be suspicious if someone else tried to join with a political platform that looked exactly like mine.

I wrote this chapter to further show how the Logos Party should work. I am submitting some of my current political beliefs for public scrutiny. I want all of my views challenged and the false or weak ideas in my worldview exposed, and I am not capable of finding all the weaknesses on my own. I am confident there are weaknesses in the personal views I am about to explain, and I truly long for people of different views to help expose those weaknesses. I will not be offended, but, on the contrary, will be grateful. My goal is a worldview that consists of nothing but truth. That is how a person of reason thinks. That is how a Logosan thinks.

To more easily explain my political platform, I like to view it through the lens of the 7 E's: enlightenment, education, economy, environment, energy, equality and enemies. I think a person's entire political platform can fit within these seven categories.[38]

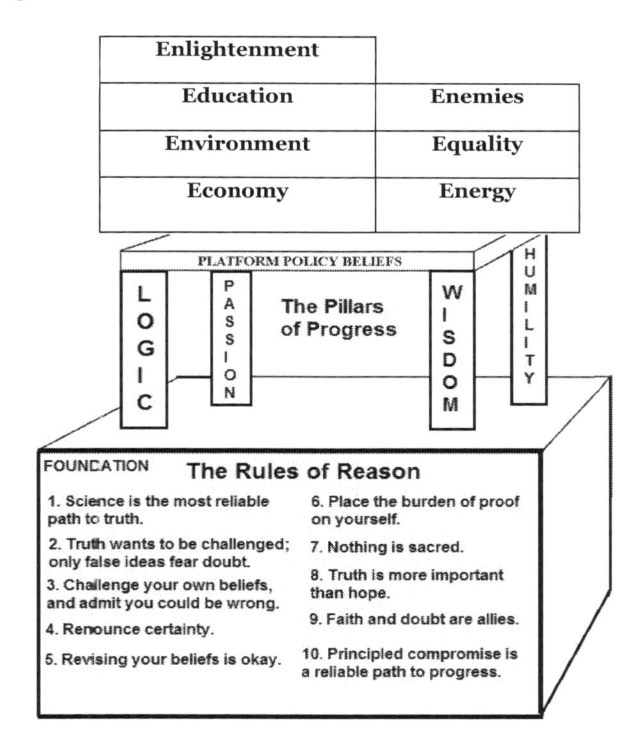


[38] For the sake of space, this is only a general summary of my platform within each E.

## The Seven E's

### 1. Enlightenment

Centered in Europe, the movement known as "The Enlightenment" took place largely in the 18th century. This movement focused on many ideas: some were liberty, tolerance, free speech, constitutional government and the separation of church and state. I believe all of these ideas revolved around the idea that reason and science are the best sources of knowledge. That is why the Enlightenment is also known as the "Age of Reason."

In the early seventeenth century, the work of Rene Descartes and Francis Bacon laid the foundation for Enlightenment thinking. Descartes and his method of extreme doubt helped show us the first phase of reason of how difficult it is to find truth, and Bacon's formulation of the scientific method showed us the second phase of reason, the method of how to find truth.

Then, in the late 17th century, Isaac Newton's book *Principia* challenged traditional thinking about science. His laws of gravity and motion redefined the nature of the world in natural laws that could be tested. This paved the way for revolutions in science throughout the 18th, 19th, and 20th centuries.

Also during this time, John Locke challenged traditional political thinking. He claimed that people had the right to challenge and change the government if it did not protect natural rights to life, liberty and property. His work helped pave the way for political revolutions throughout the 18th and 19th centuries.

During the Enlightenment, Benjamin Franklin traveled to Europe many times. While there, he engaged in the scientific and political debates. Then, he brought new enlightenment ideas back to America. Thomas Jefferson also followed the Enlightenment ideas spreading throughout Europe, later incorporating those ideas into the Declaration of Independence. James Madison also read many of the great Enlightenment thinkers and infused their ideas into the United States Constitution. In other words, I believe Enlightenment principles centered around reason are the foundational principles on which the Founding Fathers of the United States formed America's liberal democracy.

Enlightenment principles may, in part, sound like the Rules of Reason, which would mean that the foundation of the Logos Party is also part of my political platform, and that would be true. They are that important. Improving the health of democracy is the goal of the Logos Party, it is part of my platform, and, though I could be wrong, Enlightenment principles are key to improving the health of democracy. The goal is to remind America that the United States was founded on Enlightenment thinking, and following those principles are the best health practices for the body of a liberal democracy.

## 2. Education

I think progress is dependent on constantly improving a democracy's education system. According to many international tests, over the course of the last few decades the United States' education system has gradually fallen in rank across science, mathematics and literacy, [39] a trend that has almost paralleled the United States' fall in rank on the Democracy Index.

[39] In 1990, the US ranked sixth in the world for its levels of education — dozens of spots ahead of where it was in 2018.

That might be a coincidence, or it might be connected. If true, then maybe if the education system is improved, then so also the health of democracy would be improved. As Thomas Jefferson wrote, "If a nation wants to be ignorant and free, it wants what never was and will never be."[40]

Though, according to international tests, the United States' education system is ranked much lower than it used to be, I also think that a test may not be able to evaluate creativity, ambition, and risk-taking, traits necessary for success in science, the arts and entrepreneurial fields. Maybe other countries are better than the United States at producing great test takers, but I wonder if those students are as creative of thinkers as students in the United States. Maybe they are or maybe they are not, but I don't think current tests are good at determining an answer to this question.

I think the "teach to the test" mentality often found in public schools because of the incessant focus on standardized tests can churn out students who may be good at memorizing information, but have not learned how to think critically. I believe success in the global market, global society, and life in general is less about memorization and more about the ability to think creatively. So, though memorization is important, I think classes should focus more on training students to be critical thinkers that challenge conventional thinking. Make them into innovators instead of memorization machines. We have computers to do that. Private schools seem to be

[40] Jefferson wrote this line in a letter to Charles Yancey on January 6, 1816.

better at this because they are not tied to standardized tests.

I believe there should be policy reform that provides more equal funding to schools across all locations. I believe that this funding should also focus on tailoring curricula to fit the student instead of expecting each student to adapt to the curriculum. In other words, I think the education system in public schools should be flexible enough that each student is able to progress at the pace of their abilities, instead of a one-size-fits all structure that forces kids to try and learn at the same speed. I think there should be a greater focus on civics education because it helps to create both a greater understanding of the political system and a greater appreciation for the rights and freedoms that system provides.

From my own life, I believe experience is by far a better educator than sitting in a classroom. I learned far more about what I wanted to do in the year after college, during which time I traveled the country as the personal assistant to an author and speaker (and was paid for it), than I did the four years of college (that I paid for). I learned more about international politics during my deployment as a paid public affairs officer in Kosovo than I did the two years of grad school I paid to earn a masters in global politics. So I think education should place a greater focus on experience than classroom instruction.

### 3. Environment

The environment is everything. It is the water we drink, the air we breathe, the food we eat, the forest we hike through, the animals we hear at night and see in the wilderness, our entire body, the entire universe, and even the thoughts we think. Everything.

I believe that earth's climate is growing hotter and, if it continues, will have long-term negative consequences for mankind. I think the earth will be fine. Mother Nature has gone through major climate changes that have caused mass extinctions before and she is still here. She may look different, but she will be fine. It is mankind that should worry. We shouldn't want to take better care of the environment for the sake of the earth, but for own sake. Mother Nature may one day decide that she has had enough of humans and go through a detox just like the one she went through 65 million years ago.

I believe mankind plays a major role in the changing climate, and I believe mankind can help reverse the damage. But, even if drastic changes must be made and made quickly in the next decade, I think that any proposal has to garner widespread acceptance. So, if the extreme proposal—something like all carbon producing cars off the roads in the next decade—is being rejected by the majority, then, instead of no progress being made, a more moderate proposal should be presented that can gain widespread acceptance so that we can at least keep moving forward. As moderate proposals are accepted, more moderate proposals can be presented, and so on and so on, so that the drastic changes mankind has to make are accepted in small doses.

People will argue that this kind of approach will still bring a pending climate crisis. But what is better: that progress continues to be stalemated because radical shifts cannot gain widespread acceptance and therefore never get implemented, or that more moderate programs are implemented so that we are at least moving forward with the hope of eventually achieving everything in the extreme proposal that could not get passed?

Taking care of the environment requires long-term thinking. Taking care of the environment requires the entire planet to be good at long-term planning, since the pollution of one country affects every other country. Besides improving education, taking care of the environment should be priority number one.

## 4. Economy

If the environment is everything, the economy is every part of society: where we live, how we live, our college choice, our career choice, relationships and marriage, having children, how we plan our lives, how we eat, how we rest, and what we constantly think about. As I write this, I am sitting in a coffee shop in Munich, Germany. I am thinking about the economy, not on a global or national scale, but about whether I have enough Euro in my wallet, how much train tickets cost, should I buy another cup of coffee, was going to the Eagle's Nest worth the money since it was so foggy I couldn't see the view of the Alps, et cetera, et cetera. The economy is everything within society, and almost everything we think about.

I believe in free market capitalism. But I don't think the free market should be completely free. I believe in Adam Smith's invisible hand that guides the economy, but that hand should be given parameters within in which it can freely move the economy, parameters that help do things like reign in corruption and prevent monopolies. I believe that a completely socialistic society is bad for progress, but I think a balance of socialism and capitalistic principles (similar to what we already have) may be the best option—not for all time, but for our current times.

I believe debt usually causes more negatives than positives, and should be avoided in almost all circumstances. I think the flat tax where everybody gets taxed the same percentage of their income or business revenue regardless of their income or profit is the most democratic tax system. No matter what people say is their most important platform issue, I believe the economy is everybody's most important issue. I believe the most basic principle of economics is that people have unlimited wants, but there are limited resources. It is this delicate balance that everybody must try to manipulate in order to support their platform issues.

### 5. Energy

The environment is everything, the economy is every part of society, and everything requires energy. Therefore, energy is the main focus of both the environmental and economic policy. I believe there needs to be a gradual overhaul in the systems of how the world acquires energy: from how we power motorized vehicles, to how we produce food, to the food we eat to give us energy. All options should be on the table, including continued but better use of fossil fuels, hydro power, solar power, and nuclear power. I admit that for all of my life, knowingly and unknowingly, I have been part of the problem. But I think I am willing to take on the discomforts that a transition in how we obtain and use energy may incur.

## 6. Equality

Equality encompasses all social interactions. Civil equality should subject us to the same laws and grant us the same rights with no discrimination based on religion, belief, race or social status. Political equality should include universal suffrage, the right to form political parties, contest elections, and have access to all offices. Social equality implies that all citizens should enjoy the same opportunities, aside from the privileges in which a particular person may have been born into that give them more or less opportunities than others. Natural equality implies that all are born free and equal, and the state should seek to reduce inequality. Finally, economic equality implies that every citizen should at least have the basics of life fulfilled to prevent them from falling into poverty. These five types of equality are more general explanations of specific types of equality, such as gender equality and racial equality. Equal justice under the law is the most important type of equality.

I believe equality should be sought in a general sense that no race, gender, or class is treated better than any other. I believe there should be equality of belief in the sense that there is freedom of religion and non-religion, but this freedom of belief should not exempt any system of belief from scrutiny. “Truth fears no trial,” so if any belief system thinks it provides truth then it should welcome the world’s scrutiny and should not want any kind of legal protection or social contract that forbids it from being challenged.

I believe if people of the same sex want to get married, they should be allowed to. I believe marriage is an honorable institution, but it is not necessary for every couple. I believe the death penalty should be outlawed. I believe if life has been created, regardless of the circumstances in which it was created, it should be given the chance to live. That said, I don't think abortion should be outlawed: each woman should choose for themselves. I believe women can do any job a man can—whether the job is physical, intellectual, creative, or leadership (unless the job specifically requires biological specifics to carry out). Women should be equally compensated for doing the same job as their masculine counterparts.

I believe every country has the right to guard its borders and place strict limitations on who is allowed in and out of their country, but those standards should not be based on race or wealth.

I believe healthcare should be considered a right for all citizens. Idealistically, I would like healthcare to cost more for those who have bad health habits. But that probably is not realistic. There should be a private option, and a greater focus on preventative measures.

Finally, I believe humans are no better than animals, and humans ourselves are a type of animal. Yes, humans are better than any animal at certain things, but animals also have abilities they are better at than humans.

### 7. Enemies

The final E refers to national security. I believe national security is comprised of defense, diplomacy, and development. As far as defense, I believe in having a strong military that is rarely, if ever, called upon to fight. I believe a person's fitness to be a soldier should be measured based on character, competence, and conditioning. The focus should be more on better soldiers instead of more soldiers. There should be a system by which soldiers can turn down missions without punishment if they think the mission is for an unjust cause.

National security should include an equal focus on diplomacy and international development. Helping make other countries who are well-governed more economically secure— such as helping them expand rights and opportunities for women—makes that country safer, which in turn makes the United States and the world safer. I believe no country acts selflessly, and almost everything a country does on the international scene, no matter how good for another country it is, is ultimately done to help improve its own economy or national security.

I believe there is no such thing as eternal allies or eternal enemies. Today's enemy might be tomorrow's ally and vice versa, so every country should be treated with both respect and suspicion. A country can be an ally on one issue and an enemy on another. For example, two countries can work together on oil, one buying and one selling, while at the same time one country condemns the human rights practices of the other country. I also believe that no country is forever weak or forever strong. For that reason each country should be treated with respect and equality, because the weak may one day be as strong or stronger than us. I believe war is the epitome of ignorance, but in very select cases some types of peace are not better than war.

I think countries should mingle with affairs of other countries very carefully because in trying to fix the world we could make things worse. Resources should be devoted to preventing the use of nuclear weapons, but I think the threat of nuclear war is exaggerated for political gains. I believe space travel is a worthwhile endeavor, and it is best done through a regulated private sector.

**Conclusion**

If you read my seven E's and conclude you do not want to be a member because you disagree with one or more of my beliefs or you conclude you want to be a member because you agree with many of my views, then you are missing the point of the Logos Party. You do not join because you agree with other member's platforms. You join because you agree with the Rules of Reason and the Pillars of Progress, and because you value intellectual diversity because it helps lead to truth.

Every view of mine that I described has changed over the years, and, because my rim is raised high out of certainty's reach, I continue to challenge my own views, which will probably cause more changes. That is what a person of reason who cares about truth more than their opinion of the truth does. I have great conviction in the credibility of each view within my platform, but because of the standard of reason my views are held to, some of them or all of them may change more in the future, either in whole or in part. To many, being willing to admit I could be wrong on that widespread and thorough of a level itself sounds like weakness. On the contrary, I think it sounds like strength. This way I continue to challenge my worldview and see it as a work in progress.

Because my views are subject to being changed, does that mean I am wishy-washy or indecisive about what I believe? No. It means I am intellectually honest with myself about the vast limits to my knowledge in every area of study. I stand strongly on my platform views, but I don't forget those views are built on the Rules of Reason and the Pillars of Progress, which demand that I am intellectually honest with myself.

My beliefs have met enough of the burden of proof, closing the canyon of doubt enough, so I am willing to allow my bridge of faith to take me the rest of the way to believe in them. But none of my views have met the burden of proof enough that they can dunk on the standard of certainty, and none of them ever will, because the rim will always be raised out of certainty's reach.

Picture the following six ideas within a pyramid. This pyramid is the *pyramid of preservation.*

5. Platform
4. Democracy
3. First Amendment
2. Human rights, rule of law,
equal justice under the law
1. Reason/Enlightenment principles

Number 5, one's platform views, is the top of the pyramid. In the order of preservation, my platform views are the least important and the first thing I would sacrifice. Then, in order of least important to most important would be democracy, First Amendment rights, human rights and the rule of law, and the most important is reason. Notice that nowhere in this hierarchy are political parties mentioned.

None of my platform views—mentioned or unmentioned in this chapter—are more important than the foundation of reason on which they are built. No issue within national security or the economy—not the climate crisis or the importance of energy transition—are more important than the idea that reason raises the standard of evidence beyond certainty's reach so that there is always room for doubt, because progress on all of my platform views requires reason.

# Chapter Eight
# The Logosan Citizen

The question I try to answer in this chapter is: *What does a reason-based party look like in action for different members within a democratic society?* The specific roles I will briefly explain are voter, journalist, and political candidate.

## Voter

Before voting, a Logosan does their homework on the candidates and initiatives. To be an informed voter, a Logosan is intentional about being exposed to a diversity of opinions, especially views that challenge their own, in order to avoid falling into an echo chamber where they only see and hear information they agrees with. In deciding who to vote for, a Logosan focuses as much, if not more, on a candidate's decision-making process as they do on the decisions that candidate makes.

Once in office, unforeseen circumstances often arise that cause some components of a candidate's campaign platform to no longer be the best option. In those moments, a Logosan wants a person in office who operates from a foundation of open-minded, ruthless reason. That elected official's decision-making process allows for their policy views to adapt with new circumstances. A Logosan votes for candidates who cannot only handle criticism, but who want constructive criticism from the media, opponents, and especially the voters.

There are people who vote for a particular party's candidate, no matter who that person is or what they believe. That seems like party dogma at its worst. One of the goals of the Logos Party is to break the mindset of voting more for a party instead of a candidate. The Logos Party believes the candidate, their platform, and decision-making process should be a voter's focus, and not that candidate's party. In other words, the Logos Party wants the electorate to vote for candidates. Not a party.

## Journalist

A Logosan who is a journalist, regardless of what media outlet they work for, holds themselves to the standards of the *NNN: Neutral News Network*. A Logosan journalist may have strong opinions, but they try to be neutral or unbiased in their reporting, unless producing a product that is clearly designated as an opinion piece. They refuse to intentionally produce propaganda. They compete against other journalists, yes, by trying to obtain a story first. But also, and more importantly, they compete by being the most accurate in the telling of the story, even if the truth challenges the credibility of their own views. The central purpose of journalism is to provide citizens with accurate information to help them operate in a free society. To help journalism fulfill that purpose, the nine core principles that follow have become generally accepted as a definitive standard of what good journalism looks like.

1. Journalism's first obligation is to the truth.
2. Journalism's first loyalty is to citizens.

3. Journalism's essence is discipline of verification.
4. Journalism's practitioners must maintain independence from those they cover.
5. Journalism must serve as an independent monitor of power.
6. Journalism must provide a forum for public criticism and compromise.
7. Journalism must strive to make the significant interesting and relevant.
8. Journalism must keep the news comprehensive and proportional.
9. Journalism's practitioners must be allowed to exercise their personal conscience.

**Candidate**

Logosans are welcomed and encouraged to run for office. While campaigning, they should make a clear distinction between the Logos Party's foundation of the Rules of Reason and Pillars of Progress (which is the same for all members) and their personal campaign platform, which are their personal beliefs and not official Logos Party views. The Logos Party has no official stance on any policy issue.

A Logos Party candidate should campaign with strong conviction in their platform views, but they should balance that conviction by expressing a desire for their views to be challenged and possibly changed. While delivering speeches and debating other candidates, it will be tempting for a Logos Party candidate to exhibit dogmatic tendencies. If a Logos Party candidate persists in dogmatic certainty, and, when confronted about it, refuses to humble their mind before reason and express open-mindedness, they will probably be asked to leave the pride of the

Logos Party. They are no longer acting like a reason roaring Lion of Logic.

The audience of a Logosan candidate's campaign rally could be made up of people from the entirety of the country, spanning region, race, religion, or identity. The reason the audience of a Logosan candidate could be so diverse is because everyone who is a supporter of the Logosan candidate would submit to the idea that reason is more important than their differences and their political views. Intellectual diversity is one of the greatest sources of power. It would be an audience of thousands of independent thinkers with different platforms. It would be a *reason rally.*

**Two Conversations**

Picture two different conversations.

The first conversation consists of five different Congressman. Each is a representative from one of five different political parties: one from a far-left party, one from a left-center party, one from a centrist party, one from a right-center party, and one from a far-right party. The five congressmen walk into Independence Hall in Philadelphia, enter the Assembly Room, and sit down around a table.

They talk for two hours. Their conversation covers the topics of abortion, gun rights, national security, climate change, taxes, the economy, education, Chinese and Russian relations, and Middle Eastern policy. Each of the five political parties represented in this conversation create a platform of policies that all members are expected to support. Each of these five representatives feels an obligation to defend their party's platform and try to persuade the other four parties to their views. In order to accomplish this goal, each feels that they cannot compromise on any party stance. Each tries to dominate the conversation, competing to see who can argue best.

They barely listen to each other. When they do listen, they are mostly trying to figure out how best to counter one another's arguments. Each party wishes they were the only party in the country. Even on issues where they have widespread agreement, they focus on their differences and amplify those parts to try and maintain a clear ideological division from all other parties. They do not seek to find common ground, cordially discussing their differences. At the end of the conversation, all five Congressmen walk out of Independence Hall believing more strongly in the righteousness of their party's platform views than they did when they walked in.

For the second conversation, the same five Congressmen sit in the Assembly Room. They are Group A. Then, five other Congressmen (Group B) walk into the Assembly Room and sit down between each member of Group A. Each Congressmen in Group B represent a different platform, the full spectrum of thought from far-left to far-right. But instead of each congressman representing a different party, Group B are all independents (or maybe Logosans).

Group B asks Group A if they can start their conversation by reading a few things. Group A reluctantly allows it. Someone from Group B then reads Benjamin Franklin's final speech, which was delivered in that same room at the end of the Constitutional Convention, because the speech exemplifies a commitment to intellectual humility, principled compromise, and ability to remain open-minded. Someone else reads the definition of constructive criticism. Someone else reads the section in chapter two on the biggest misconception about reason. Someone else reads the Logos Party short explanation of reason mentioned at the end of chapter two:

> A person of reason sets the standard of evidence beyond certainty's reach so that there is always room for doubt and never room for certainty. Since there is always room for doubt, they are intellectually humble and admit they could be wrong, challenge their own views, welcome others challenging their beliefs, and see their worldview as a work that is always in progress, so their mind is forever open to being changed.

All five members of Group B then say the United States' founding motto, "E Pluribus Unum: Out of many, one." They introduce their time together by reciting all of these different things to remind themselves that the atmosphere of their conversation should reflect that of the culture of the Constitutional Convention that took place in that room.

The ten congressmen then begin their discussion. Their conversation covers the topics of abortion, gun rights, national security, climate change, taxes, the economy, education, Chinese relations and Russian relations, and Middle Eastern policy.

Each Congressman in Group B has strong opinions like the Congressmen in Group A, but, because they are people who set their standard of evidence beyond certainty's reach so that there is always room for doubt, they believe reason is more important than their platforms. They checked dogma at the door and are willing to admit they could be wrong. They challenge their own views, welcome the challenges of others, and see their worldview as a work in progress. Though their talk is sometimes combative, it is all the time respectful.

At the end of the conversation, each of the ten Congressmen understand better the others' perspectives because the presence of reason created a more cordial conversation of principled compromise. Group A may have resented the influx of reason and appreciation of intellectual diversity by Group B, but maybe they felt a little convicted by their presence. No one in Group A may have been influenced to modify their own views, but the next time the conversation consists of only Group A, maybe there will be a little more reason, a little more willingness to compromise, and a little more appreciation of intellectual diversity.

## Chapter Nine

## The Logosan Leader

2,400 years ago, in Plato's *Republic,* Socrates said, "Until philosophers rule as kings in their cities...cities will have no rest from evils." The Philosopher-King is Plato's ideal leader. The four cardinal virtues of a Philosopher-King are moderation, wisdom, courage, and justice. They have a good character, a calm disposition, and a sound mind. Above all, the Philosopher-King is dedicated to knowledge. Probably the most notable example of a Philosopher-King was Marcus Aurelius, the Roman Emperor from 161 CE to 180 CE.

Similar to the Philosopher-King, a Logosan leader is dedicated to truth above all else. In everything the Logosan leader does, they are a wisdom-loving, truth-seeking, lifelong learner. The difference between the Philosopher-King and the Logosan Leader is that the Philosopher-King is a benevolent dictator who makes all the decisions because they are the only one trusted. They are the most intelligent, making decisions with the good of the people in mind. Meanwhile, the Logosan Leader leads within a democratic framework where they build a team of experienced, talented and dedicated people from diverse backgrounds and facilitate a culture of intellectually diverse collaboration. They create an intellectual laboratory where all ideas are welcome to be tested. In other words, the Logosan leader is the wisest and best person to lead because they *don't* think they have all the answers, and so rely on the expertise of a diverse followership. They are decisive, but open-mindedly so. They set clear goals, but remain flexible in their methods, and their goals are open to revision.

Probably the most notable example of a Logosan leader is George Washington when he served as president of the Constitutional Convention in the summer of 1787. During the convention Washington didn't talk much in comparison with many of the other fifty-five delegates. He at times voiced his opinion, but I think Washington saw his role as more of one who facilitated and maintained a fertile atmosphere of intellectual diversity: tamping down tempers when they arose and ensuring that delegates checked their dogma at the door so that the debates remained somewhat cordial, open-minded, and reason-based.

I once had to teach a leadership class in the military. I used the opportunity to develop and write out my personal leadership philosophy. What resulted was the *15 C's of leadership*.[41] This goes beyond focusing only on being a person of reason who is dedicated to intellectual diversity. This list is not comprehensive so there might be traits not listed that would also be good for a leader to possess.

## The 15 C's of Leadership

### 1. Character

Good character is the most important leadership trait. A leader's example is their greatest tool. A Logosan leader is honest, but they are tactful in their truth-telling. People of character follow people of character.

[41] I have not changed any of the 15 C's, but I have adapted some of the descriptions to better reflect a Logosan leader.

Character is more important than knowledge and talent. A Logosan leader is honest with everybody, and transparent with most.

### 2. Competence

Character is foundational to good leadership, but people will not follow incompetence. A Logosan leader understands the limits of their knowledge, and they are a lifelong learner. Competence listens to others. A Logosan leader understands that they do not have all the answers, and they are great at asking questions. A Logosan leader understands their job and has a general understanding of everyone else's job. They try to lead people smarter than they are and learn from them.

### 3. Courage

People follow character and competence. They are inspired by courage. Courage is not the absence of fear, but acting despite fear. A good leader puts themselves where courage is needed. They have the courage to lead into the unfamiliar. Courage is not a character trait, but the foundation of all character, especially at its testing point.

### 4. Conviction

Courage is inspiring. Conviction is contagious. A Logosan leader has strong beliefs, but one of their greatest convictions is that they will have no conviction that is ever beyond the possibility of being changed. They know the difference between conviction and dogmatism. They help others do what they love, understanding that people will have greater conviction and passion if they enjoy their work.

## 5. Compromise

A Logosan leader understands that much of what they believe is probably false, so they challenge their own views more than they challenge others. They are firm in their goals, but flexible in the means to achieving them. They define the parameters of their tolerance with subordinates, and are willing to bend to keep from breaking. They understand the difference between principled compromise and cowardly compromise.

## 6. Compassion

A Logosan leader learns the stories of those they lead so they can better empathize with them. They take on the pain and burdens of those they lead. They seek to improve the lives of those they lead. They understand that advancing others advances themselves. They own blame and share praise.

## 7. Change

A Logosan leader cultivates a culture of change. If something isn't working, they change it. If something is working, they improve it. Their subordinates feel comfortable taking the initiative and enacting change.

## 8. Completion of the mission

A Logosan leader praises effort, but remains focused on results. They attract those that are driven to accomplish the mission. They are solution conscious. They expect obstacles and are determined to break through them. They are resilient, quickly bouncing back from failure.

### 9. Calculation

A Logosan leader plans thoroughly. They understand that the element of chance is always present, but they leave as little to chance as they can. They create a plan A and plan B, but probably also a plan C.

### 10. Communication

A Logosan leader is clear and concise. they simplify the message. They understand that they can say more if they can say it with less words. They stay on message, but are flexible in how they communicate that message. They are a good listener. They study their audience before trying to communicate with them. They regularly repeat their message.

### 11. Creativity

A Logosan leader is a visionary, helping people see what cannot be seen. They see potential problems before they arise. They cultivate a culture of creativity where people feel comfortable presenting original, innovative, and uncomfortable ideas.

### 12. Composure

A leader's presence is the first thing people notice. A Logosan leader is calm, especially in the midst of chaos. If they are going to get mad, then they get mad on purpose. They project confidence, but understand the difference between confidence and cockiness.

### 13. Consistency

People can more easily follow consistency than unpredictability. A Logosan leader sets clear standards and holds themselves and those they lead to those standards. People are not always wondering how the Logosan leader will react. The Logosan leader understands that change can be good, but especially change within the framework of consistent standards.

### 14. Comedy

A Logosan leader works hard, but doesn't take themselves too seriously. They have found a balance between contentment and discontentment. They laugh regularly.

### 15. Collaboration

A Logosan leader finds good people, provides the vision, and then serves their people. They know when to follow, and create a culture where they value constructive criticism. One of their greatest functions as a leader is to produce more leaders so the Logosan leader shares responsibility.

# CONCLUSION

## The Graveyard of Governments

I went live with the Logos Party website the morning of July 4, 2019. That afternoon, I went to the president's *Salute to America* celebration at the Lincoln Memorial. My status as a White House appointee allowed me to get close to the stage. Twenty-two days later, on July 26, I was fired by the White House.

The morning of the firing, I arrived at work before 08:00. When I opened my work email, I saw a message from my boss that had been sent shortly after 06:00 AM with a simple subject heading that read something like "09:45 Meeting my office, Mandatory." That was all it said, but I immediately understood it probably meant I was about to be let go.

I spent the next hour sending emails to my personal email with everything attached that I wanted off of my government computer. (I correctly assumed that when I walked into my boss's office at 09:45 I was never again logging back into that computer.)

I was given the option to resign or be terminated. I hesitated to sign the resignation letter because part of me wanted the record to show that I was fired by the White House. I eventually signed the letter and took the benefits that come with resigning.

It will show that the White House let me go because "my position was no longer needed." That could be true, but the timing seemed too coincidental. My firing took place three weeks after I went live with a new (somewhat satirical) party and did a couple interviews on big radio stations. It also seemed too coincidental that a few days before I was let go, I received an email from a producer explaining how wrong they thought it was that—even though it wasn't open for membership—I would create a new political party while working for the White House. They threatened to contact the White House press office, but said they wouldn't. I think they did.

Though I could be wrong, I think the reason for my firing was because of the Logos Party, which is guided by principles that the administration probably disagreed with. The truth is that I wanted to leave that job many months earlier. The only reason I stayed as long as I did was so that I could get fired by the White House in order to further the idea of the Logos Party. I thought it would be a good conclusion to this book. But I assumed it would be 2020 before I was fired. I was glad, but surprised the plan worked so fast.

After I was escorted out of the building by security, who seemed surprised by my calm demeanor, I went to the movie theater. After the movie, I went to a coffee shop. I read a little. I wrote a little. Mostly I watched people and thought about how none of them had any idea that I had just been fired by the White House. I wondered what life-changing events had just happened in their worlds that I had no idea about.

When I returned home, sitting on my front porch in scrubs and a long white lab coat was Doctor Democracy. After six months, the doctor finally decided to make another house call.

I walked up the stairs and sat next to the doctor.

"Let go today, huh?" Doctor Democracy rhetorically asked.

I nodded.

"That was quick."

I nodded again. "I expected it and wanted it, but I didn't think it would happen so fast. Now that it happened, I feel alone. The executive branch of the most powerful country in the world just fired me. I feel overwhelmed, outnumbered, and overpowered."

The doctor sat silent for a moment, slowly nodding. Then, he stood and walked down the stairs. When I didn't follow, he looked back and said, "Let's go."

I didn't ask where we were going. I just followed.

We climbed into my vehicle and drove north out of the city on US 50 East. About 40 miles later, we arrived at the Naval Academy in Annapolis. We parked and walked to the cemetery. Eventually, with the Severn River behind us, we stopped in front of a newer tombstone. It read:

John S. McCain III
29 August 1936 – 25 August 2018

After a silent moment of staring at McCain's tombstone, Doctor Democracy said, "I helped motivate you to create a reason-based political party for independent minds. You have done that. The Logos Party could be better, but it is decent. Like the Constitution and American democracy, let it always be a work in progress.

"When you were creating the Logos Party, you had confidence that you were on the right path. When the Logos Party was only a figment of your imagination, the potential persecution you might face was easily embraced because it was only a fantasy. Today you received the first real gut punch. I now wonder, you wanted the persecution when it was in your imagination, but can you handle it in reality?"

Looking at McCain's tombstone, I concluded that being fired by the White House was nothing compared to what he went through as a prisoner of war in Vietnam. I nodded as I looked at the doctor. "Yes, I think I can handle it. Being fired by the White House should not discourage me, but instead should strengthen me. I think I just need the weekend to catch my breath from this first gut punch."

The doctor chuckled and nodded. "That's fair." He scanned the cemetery. "While you catch your breath, take a second look at that tombstone."

To my shock, it was no longer John McCain's. Instead, it read:

United States' Democracy

1789—

On either side of the United States' tombstone was a gravestone for the ancient Greek and Roman republics. I scanned the suddenly transformed cemetery. Each tombstone was a different dead empire. Ancient Egypt. Mesopotamia. The Akkadian Empire. The Persian Empire. The Qing Dynasty. The Russian Empire. The Mongol Empire. The Ottoman Empire. There were hundreds.

"This is the *graveyard of governments*." The doctor looked at the United States' tombstone. "After the Constitution went into effect, some of the Founding Fathers reserved this plot because they thought the new country they helped form would have a short life. John Adams wrote, 'Democracy never lasts long. It soon wastes, exhausts, and murders itself. There is never a democracy that did not commit suicide.'[42] He was speaking for many of the Founders. Most of them would be surprised that the United States has lasted this long.

"One of the main reasons the Founding Fathers feared that the democracy they created would eventually kill itself is because they feared the rise of dogmatic parties. John Adams also wrote, 'There is nothing which I dread so much as a division of the republic into two great parties. This is to be dreaded as the greatest political evil under our Constitution.'[43] Alexander Hamilton wrote, 'We are attempting, by this Constitution, to abolish factions, and to unite all parties for the general welfare."[44]

Shaking his head, Doctor Democracy smirked. "Ironically, each of those men, once the Constitution was implemented, would within only a few years help create the first political party, the Federalists. In response, Jefferson and Madison, also two founders who previously spoke against party factions, created the Democratic-Republican Party. Instead of either being a reason-based party like the party-before-parties atmosphere of the Constitutional Convention, those two parties helped create the framework for the dogmatic platform-based two-party system.

"Like Plato's theory of the forms, the Founding Fathers created the Constitution as a blueprint for what they thought the ideal government looked like. Human nature can corrupt anything, no matter how idealistic the blueprint. The Founding Fathers understood this. For that reason, they used some of

---

[42] Adams wrote this line in a letter to John Taylor on December 17, 1814.

[43] Adams wrote this line in a letter to Jonathan Jackson on October 2, 1780.

[44] Hamilton said this line on June 25, 1788 in the convention of the State of New York on the Adoption of the Federal Constitution.

human nature's best principles, the principles of the Enlightenment, to create a government system built to keep in check the worst parts of human nature, the top of that list being human nature's dogmatic tendencies.

"Many of the Founders shared the idea that a partisan two-party system was the worst thing that could happen to the new idealistic government they created, but then they succumbed to the very vice they once spoke against. Thus was the creation of political parties that morphed into the dogmatic two-party system that is the cause for almost all of democracy's health problems. The Logos Party is the form, your idealistic blueprint of what a party of reason looks like. But, if you ever decide to take it out of the theoretical and turn it into a real party, like the Constitution, it can become corrupted. Like the Founding Fathers, *you* can be corrupted.

"James Madison wrote, 'Since the general civilization of mankind, I believe there are more instances of the abridgement of freedom of the people by gradual and silent encroachments by those in power than by violent and sudden usurpations.'[45] It is good that the Logosan Creed says, 'Democracy's survival largely depends on each citizen protecting themselves from dogma's subtle invasions,' because if the Logos Party becomes corrupted it will probably happen inch by inch. So, guard the edges where dogma likes to nibble off an inch of reason at a time."

The doctor cupped his ear and said, "Hear the lions of logic roar in the distance? There are many of them, all over America and the world. They need to hear a roar of reason that is loud enough to make

[45] Madison delivered this line in a speech in Virginia's ratifying convention on control of the Military on June 16, 1788.

them all aware that they are not alone, a roar that can unify them to roar reason more as one."

A roar sounded. I turned. Out of the Severn River walked a wet lion of logic.[46] He stood next to me and roared again.

In the distance, what sounded like a whole pride began roaring reason in unison. It sounded beautiful.

Once the roaring stopped, Doctor Democracy said, "I am the collective conscious of the great political and philosophical minds of history. We worked hard, we wrote hard, we fought hard, and we risked much for the cause of reason, humanism, justice, and democracy. Our ideas can help save democracy, but only if the living keep them alive through reading them again, teaching them again, fighting for them again, living them again, roaring them again. Saving America's democracy is not on me. It is on you, and every American citizen. You are Doctor Democracy."

The doctor looked into the distance at the setting sun, now split by the horizon. He put his hand over his eyes to block some of the light. "Throughout the Constitutional Convention, I often saw Ben Franklin look at the carved sun split by the horizon on the back of George Washington's chair. He said he often wondered if it was rising or setting. As delegates signed the Constitution, Franklin happily said that it was a rising sun."[47]

The doctor looked at American democracy's tombstone. "Today, Franklin might look at American

---

[46] Or, for the sake of the metaphor, the Severn River was now the River of Reason that the Lion of Logic walked out of.
[47] James Madison is credited with writing that Franklin said this to him at the end of the Convention.

democracy's declining health and say that the sun is setting as the darkness of dogma is pushing back the light of logic. He might say that a rededication to the principles that guided the party before parties at the Constitutional Convention is necessary for the sun to rise again. He might say we need the principles of reason, intellectual diversity, and principled compromise embodied in the Logos Party."

Doctor Democracy closed his eyes, silently soaking up the warmth of the light of logic. I closed my eyes as well. I envisioned all the events of the last seven months from the government shutdown to being fired by the White House that morning. I was nervous. But I was ready, and I believed the Logos Party provided the remedy to American democracy's declining health.

I opened my eyes.

The cemetery was gone.

The lion was gone.

Doctor Democracy was gone.

I was sitting on my front porch.

I walked inside, sat at my desk, and began writing this book.

## Appendix

A. The Six Types of Political Conversations
B. The Logosan Creed
C. Ben Franklin's Final Speech
D. Everywhere this Book was Worked On

## A. The Six Types of Political Conversations

Our political discussions usually only cover the issues within our platforms like the economy, healthcare, national security, equal rights, or the second amendment. The Logos Party teaches that when talking politics, it would be good to begin by briefly discussing the foundation on which we build our political beliefs. People might not even realize what foundation they are using to support their platform, so emphasizing this topic at the beginning of a conversation could help bring awareness to the issue and create a more productive dialogue once the talk transitions to platform issues.

Political discussions do not break down because of differences of opinion. They break down because of the foundations on which those differences of opinion are built. The foundation on which we place our platform could be made up of dogma, reason or a combination of both. From that basis, in a political discussion between two people there are six different foundational interactions that could take place.

1. Dogma vs. Dogma
2. Dogma vs. Dogma/Reason
3. Dogma vs. Reason
4. Dogma/Reason versus/with Dogma/Reason
5. Reason versus/with Dogma/Reason
6. Reason with Reason

Reason has one purpose: get us to truth. Reason is the mind's ability to break down barriers between ignorance and truth. To break down those barriers, a person of reason raises the standard of evidence beyond certainty's reach so that there is always room for doubt and never room for certainty. That means that no matter how much evidence is discovered, a truth is never proven beyond all doubt. Since there is always room for doubt, there is always room to challenge—exactly what truth wants. Only false ideas fear doubt. Raising the standard of evidence beyond certainty's reach causes a person of reason to be intellectually humble. Intellectually humble persons exhibit five traits:[48]

1. They admit room for doubt, and leave no room for certainty.
2. They admit that they could be wrong.
3. They challenge their own beliefs.
4. They welcome other people challenging their beliefs.
5. They see their worldview as a work in progress, so their mind is open to being changed.

These are characteristics of a person that cares about truth.

In contrast, dogma is the mind's ability to build barriers to protect our opinion of the truth. To build those barriers, dogmatic people exhibit five traits:[49]

---

[48] These are an abbreviated version of the Rules of Reason.

[49] These are an abbreviated version of the Doctrines of Dogma.

1. They are certain they are right, and they have no room for doubt.
2. They are unwilling to admit they could be wrong.
3. They never challenge their own beliefs.
4. They resent other people challenging their beliefs.
5. They see their worldview as a closed system.

These are characteristics of people who care more about their opinion of the truth than the truth.

## The Six Foundational Interactions

### 1. Dogma vs. Dogma

Dogma vs. dogma is when both people in a political discussion have built their entire platform on a foundation of dogma so both people exhibit the five traits of a dogmatic mind on all of their political beliefs. There is not one political opinion that either person has on which they are willing to admit they could be wrong, wiling to challenge, welcome being challenged, or are open to their opinion being changed. These are two people who care only about their opinion of the truth on all of their views. If the goal is truth, the food and water that a healthy democracy needs, then this is the least productive interaction.

### 2. Dogma vs. Dogma/Reason

Dogma vs. dogma/reason is when one side has built its entire political platform on a foundation of dogma, and the other side has built part of its platform on dogma and part of their platform on reason. The person whose platform is built on both dogma and reason has some political views that exhibit the five traits of a dogmatic mind and some views that exhibit the traits of a person of reason.

### 3. Dogma vs. Reason

Dogma versus reason is when one side has built their entire political platform on a foundation of dogma, and the other side in the conversation has built its entire political platform on a foundation of reason.

### 4. Dogma/Reason versus/with Dogma/Reason

Dogma/reason versus/with dogma/reason is when both sides have built part of their platform on a foundation of dogma and part on a foundation of reason. Each side has political views on which it is close-minded and some views in which it is open-minded.

### 5. Reason versus/with Dogma/Reason

Reason versus/with dogma/reason is when one person in a conversation has built part of their political platform on a foundation of dogma and part of it on a foundation of reason, and the other person has built their entire political platform on a foundation of reason.

## 6. Reason with Reason

Reason-with-reason is when both people in a conversation have built their entire political platform on a foundation of reason. It is "with" instead of "versus" because, no matter how much two people disagree on platform issues, if they built their entire platform on a foundation of reason then they are on the same team. No matter how opposed the platform beliefs, for "reason-with-reason," there is no longer an "us-vs.-them" mindset. The goal is the same: truth. For reason-with-reason conversations, on every issue both people care more about truth than their opinion of the truth, so they see their entire worldview as a work in progress. No matter where they each are on the journey towards a worldview that consists of nothing but truth, they are both on the same journey, helping one another move further on that path. In a healthy democracy (in a healthy relationship of any sort) the goal is reason with reason.

***

The Logos Party's goal is for all political discourse, no matter how much two people or parties disagree, to be based on foundations of reason. When people disagree reason-with-reason is usually not human nature's natural interaction. If left to chance, we often resort to passionate dogma-versus-dogma conversations with all sides thinking they are the side of reason, but defining reason as, "If you think the way I do you are a person of reason, and if you think differently you are irrational." That is the exact opposite of how a person of reason thinks.

That is why the Logos Party is foundation-focused. The Logos Party serves as a symbol to emphasize the importance of being more intentional about focusing on the foundation underneath our platforms so that we will then be more intentional about being people of reason who have passionate reason with reason conversations.

People often hide their dogma behind a fake veneer of reason by claiming to be a person of reason without ever defining what reason looks like in practice. The Logos Party clearly defines what reason is and what reason is not to provide a standard by which we can more easily hold our political discourse intellectually accountable. By defining reason and dogma, it can become clearer to everyone what category they and others fall into. The greatest offense to most people is to be thought of as irrational. The Logos Party provides the Rules of Reason to follow to credibly avoid that label.

If at the beginning of the conversation two people are unable to agree that their interaction will involve reason-with-reason, then at least beginning the conversation this way would help all sides better understand what beliefs on which the other person is close-minded, and what beliefs (if any) on which they are open-minded. If you conclude that the other person has built an entire platform on a foundation of dogma, then you may decide to end the conversation without discussing platform issues and save yourself some time. Personally, I don't mind talking to dogma. I may be able to provide an example of intellectual humility that could plant a seed that later sprouts and breaks through the thick dam of dogma in someone's mind.

Picture this: at the beginning of every political discussion—whether it is on the floor of the Senate or the House of Representatives, a meeting in the Oval Office, diplomatic talks between heads of state, the floor of the state legislature, town halls, interviews between journalists and guests, high school and college classrooms, debate stages, or dinner tables across America—people take a moment to talk about the foundation underneath their platform in order to try to establish that the conversation will be reason with reason. Doing that at the beginning of every political discussion would serve as accountability. If during the political discussion it appears that someone has resorted to dogma, the group can refer back to the beginning of the conversation where everyone agreed that the talk was going to be reason with reason to hold the person exhibiting dogmatic tendencies accountable.

The goal of the Logos Party is to create a different kind of like-minded group. A group of people who are like-minded on a foundation of reason. Then, on that like-minded foundation, the platforms are different, creating a culture where intellectual diversity is embraced. Then, despite their different views, all would be lions of logic who roared reason.

## B. The Logosan Creed

The Logosan Creed is a concise statement of the foundational beliefs of the Logos Party.

### The Logosan Creed

In a strong democracy, I believe people vote for a candidate and not a party, citizens have independent minds, and voters study widely to be informed.

Political platforms should be built on reason; the path to progress is paved with open-mindedness, constructive criticism, and principled compromise; and the decision-making process is as important as, maybe more important than, the decisions that are made.

I believe we should learn from history, but not allow our beliefs to be imprisoned by history; democracy's survival largely depends on each citizen protecting themselves from dogma's subtle invasions.

I believe the path to truth is science and ruthless reason. Truth wants to be challenged, only false ideas fear criticism, and people who care about truth regularly challenge the credibility of their own beliefs, even the views in this creed.

## C. Ben Franklin's Speech on the Final Day of the Constitutional Convention

Ben Franklin's final speech at the Constitutional Convention embodies the ideas of the Logos Party.

Mr. President,

I confess that there are several parts of this constitution which I do not at present approve, but I am not sure I shall never approve them: For having lived long, I have experienced many instances of being obliged by better information, or fuller consideration, to change opinions even on important subjects, which I once thought right, but found to be otherwise. It is therefore that the older I grow, the more apt I am to doubt my own judgment, and to pay more respect to the judgment of others.

Most men indeed, as well as most sects in Religion, think themselves in possession of all truth, and that wherever others differ from them it is so far error. Steele a Protestant in a Dedication tells the Pope that the only difference between our Churches in their opinions of the certainty of their doctrines is, the Church of Rome is infallible, and the Church of England is never in the wrong. But though many private persons think almost as highly of their own infallibility as of that of their sect, few express it so naturally as a certain French lady, who in a dispute with her sister, said "I don't know how it happens, Sister but I meet with no body but myself, that's always in the right — Il n'y a que moi qui a toujours raison."

In these sentiments, Sir, I agree to this Constitution with all its faults, if they are such; because I think a general Government necessary for us, and there is no form of Government but what may be a blessing to the people if well administered, and believe farther that this is likely to be well administered for a course of years, and can only end in Despotism, as other forms have done before it, when the people shall become so corrupted as to need despotic Government, being incapable of any other.

I doubt too whether any other Convention we can obtain, may be able to make a better Constitution. For when you assemble a number of men to have the advantage of their joint wisdom, you inevitably assemble with those men, all their prejudices, their passions, their errors of opinion, their local interests, and their selfish views. From such an assembly can a perfect production be expected? It therefore astonishes me, Sir, to find this system approaching so near to perfection as it does; and I think it will astonish our enemies, who are waiting with confidence to hear that our councils are confounded like those of the Builders of Babel; and that our States are on the point of separation, only to meet hereafter for the purpose of cutting one another's throats. Thus I consent, Sir, to this Constitution because I expect no better, and because I am not sure, that it is not the best.

The opinions I have had of its errors, I sacrifice to the public good. I have never whispered a syllable of them abroad. Within these walls they were born, and here they shall die. If every one of us in returning to our Constituents were to report the objections he has had to it, and endeavor to gain partisans in support of them, we might prevent its being generally received, and thereby lose all the salutary effects & great advantages resulting naturally in our favor among foreign Nations as well as among ourselves, from our real or apparent unanimity.

Much of the strength & efficiency of any Government in procuring and securing happiness to the people, depends, on opinion, on the general opinion of the goodness of the Government, as well as of the wisdom and integrity of its Governors. I hope therefore that for our own sakes as a part of the people, and for the sake of posterity, we shall act heartily and unanimously in recommending this Constitution (if approved by Congress & confirmed by the Conventions) wherever our influence may extend, and turn our future thoughts & endeavors to the means of having it well administered.

On the whole, Sir, I cannot help expressing a wish that every member of the Convention who may still have objections to it, would with me, on this occasion doubt a little of his own infallibility, and to make manifest our unanimity, put his name to this instrument.

## D. Everywhere this Book was Worked On

1. Washington D.C.
    a. My House
    b. Many coffee shops
2. New York City: two coffee shops
3. Europe
    a. Germany: Munich, Nuremberg, Wittenberg, Berlin
    b. London: hotel
    c. Ferry over English Channel
    d. Paris: two coffee shops
4. Ohio
    a. Wiggin Street Coffee, Gambier
    b. Mom's house
    c. Panera Bread in Mount Vernon
5. Indiana: Camp Atterbury
6. Flights
    a. DC to Ohio; Ohio to DC
    b. DC to Atlanta; Atlanta to Munich
    c. Berlin to London
    d. Paris to Lisbon; Lisbon to DC

Senator John McCain and me in Kosovo in April of 2017. (The United States military does not endorse the Logos Party)

Made in the USA
Middletown, DE
26 October 2020